BACHELOR OF CRICKET

MIDDLE CLASS MEMOIR

SHREEDHER PRIYAN

Thanks to

Yuvraj singh

Makkal selvan Vijaysethupathi

Lyricist Vivek

Official Sponsors of the Novel "Bachelor of cricket" - Mr.Ramnath - Yuvira trends

Official Sponsors of my previous "Coded Triangles"novel

Jaya TV

Dr.Ranjith VB

United bleachers limited ,Metupalayam

Dr.Sarita

Dr.Vinitha

Dr.Madhavi

Dr.Umachamundeeswari

Thanks to my well wishers

Parivu Sakthivel

Dr.Selvakumar

Dr.Akilan

Sakkottai N Sathish kumar

Mkb studios

Olir designs

Grand pixels

Dr.Jenil Sundi Kan Vjk

Dr. Arun R kumaar

English version

Chief editor – Dr.Ranjith VB

Proof reading - Kavya Rao, Dr.Sharmila

Tamil version

Tamil translation and Editing - Dr.Nandhakumar

Translation assistance - Karthik Bala,Madhumitha baskaran

Proof reading - Sivapatham ,Sridhar G

Hindi version

Hindi translation - Mangal singh

Book Cover and Trailer team

Book Cover design - Ashik

Book cover Motion poster - GV Mediaworks

Facebook frames ,Book Posters and designs -Eswar Vijay

Trailer - Grand pixels

Direction & DOP - Dinesh Ortha

Editing - Darwin pothi

DI & VFX - Grand pixels

Associate directors -Parthiban ,Kanchana

Assistant directors- Rajesh , Sooraj

Music - Vicky Isaiamaipalan

Location courtesy - Royal school, Madurai

Nizar Khan dance academy, Madurai

My friends who are my constant support

Selva ganapathy, Arun, Raja, Viswa Janani, Anand Karthikeyan, Singaravel ,Santosh Venkataraman

My Doctor friends

Rakshaya devi, Durkha devi, Sathish kannan, Ratheesh Elangovan , Shyam , Praveen , Hari bhaskar, Adharsh, Vishnu ,Karthika, Madan, Vignesh, Sangoli, Sowmiya Annamalai, Kavin shankar, Athiban

Reviewers - Archana , Sivaranjani ,Cinebreak Tamil

Special thanks to

All my college Professors and Juniors who supported me

Contents

Contents

Somewhere something incredible is waiting to be known.

-Carl Sagan

Prologue

25/7/2020 - 7 p.m.

Even after a hectic day at work, friends compulsion to play evening cricket was not spiteful, I instantly obliged and was drained utterly by the end of the match. I had lost my shape over the past months and carrying all that extra weight left me panting. I left to my room soon because it was the day before my birthday. I had to attend the calls of everyone who would wish me at midnight.

I hit the bed by 8 p.m. I was woken violently by someone hitting my legs. I switched on the light and saw my mom struggling to speak. She was experiencing severe chest pain. For a second I was frightened by the way she was struggling to breathe.

Immediately, I gave her some tablets and took her to the nearby hospital. The intensivist took an ECG and said my mom was having a severe heart attack. As immediate intervention was needed, they referred to a higher centre. It was the peak of the Covid pandemic. I decided to take her in our own car as it was risky to take her in an ambulance.

She wasn't able to breath properly. I held her hand the entire way to the hospital and kept urging her to relax. My phone kept ringing as many were calling to wish me.I switched off the phone as I was in no mood to speak..

When we reached the hospital, she was rushed to the emergency room. After watching the ECG, the doctor said, "Your mother is in a serious condition. She has minimal chance to survive if we thrombolyse the block. Hurry up and buy this injection from the pharmacy immediately."

I ran to third floor of the hospital in the steps with my dad running behind me. I bought that injection and rushed back to the ER. I signed the form which stated the hosptial was not responsible for any complications that can arise because of the thrombolysis procedure like bleeding in the brain. I had seen many movies for getting sign in hospitals about the serious condition of the patient but signing such a form for my own mother was really a tough emotion for me to go through.

After getting the sign, the doctor started the procedure. The response for it, either good or bad, could be seen only after 30 minutes by taking ECG. My dad and I were asked to sit in the waiting room outside. I sat on a stool waiting for the next longest thirty minutes of my life to pass, all the while praying to God to save my mom's life

I was sprinting down the memory lane. My mother holding my hands as she walked me to the first day of kindergarten...The picture of her eager face peeking a glance at me while standing just outside the gates to console me as she knew I would cry... Getting me ready for the fancy dress competition during eighth grade... These images were rushing in my mind's eye. I fought back the tears waiting to escape my eyes. If I was feeling like this, then how much emotional was my father getting? We were all stressed about different things but kept it to ourselves.

CHAPTER ONE

New Expedition

Namakkal.
2010

The first day of my Higher Secondary education was starting from tomorrow.

I had packed my stuff and was set to move to a new place. One of the most threatening places to get educated, but apparently, known for helping the bright students to get some of the best possible grades in the dreaded board exams.

The quintessential Namakkal School.

Along with my parents, I finally arrived at the bus station of the town I would be staying in for the next two years.

My father and I slowly transferred my luggage from the bus on to the road and subsequently into the auto rickshaw with the help of the driver.

My mother stood by the side fretting. There were thousands of thoughts running through her mind, mostly about my future. My mind wasn't still either. It was in absolute turmoil thinking about the new place, and how my life was going to change henceforth.

We reached the school campus and found our way to the Boys hostel. I showed my Maths-Biology group admission card to the warden there.

The warden was tall and clad in khakhi. He had a telltale moustache and a hint of a beard. He was very warm to my parents. I doubted whether he would be the same way to me once my parents left.

"Welcome. I am Akmal. How are you?" the warden asked.

The usual niceties were exchanged.

"What's your name, son?" he asked me.

My mom was a typical Indian mother who answered all the questions directed towards her child.

"Shreedher Priyan", she said.

The warden smiled. And gestured us to follow him. He led us towards the staircase.

"Please walk up to the third floor and take a right. From there you room is the fourth on the left." said the warden.

My mom's eyes were already brimming with tears.

"Don't worry madam. We will take good care of your son, " he reassured my mom.

Inspite of all his reassurances, a mother's heart could seldom calm when it comes to things concerning her child.

This change would take a huge impact on my family's economy. My father had to pay ?80,000 per year for this kind of education. This was a huge amount as it used to cost less than half of that per year in other schools.

My father was very specific about what he spent his money on. It did not mean that he would regret spending his money on my schooling. yet it didn't help me get rid of the guilt either.

'I will make sure that my dad's efforts don't get wasted ' I promised myself. I made the decision to attend this school to improve my mental resilience. There was no retreating.

I entered the dormitory. It was a room for forty students with twenty double bunk cots. I always looked for comfort, and hence chose the upper bunk as it was closer to the fan. I unpacked some of my things with my mother's help and decided to do the rest later.

My mom started fussing about the small stuff as usual. "Brush your teeth. Take bath regularly. Have your meals properly. There'll be no one to take care of all that here..."

"I am not a small boy any more mom", I stopped her.

My mom was in tears by the time she had to leave. She wanted me to study in Thanjavur, my hometown. But certain things like the comfort of home had to be given up if my future was to be bright. And this was one such decision. If I saw my mother burst into tears, even I would start feeling home sick, which is why I asked my parents to leave early.

Dad said, "Don't stress yourself too much. This is another phase of life. It's a crucial couple of years, so make good friends. Try to get good marks and get placed in Anna University. I know you have crossed and survived many things in life. Just do your best. Take care of your health. That's very important."

I nodded, hugged both of them and said goodbye.

I watched them leaving. My mom turned back now and then to wave one last bye. They did not know the real reason as to why I chose to leave the comfort of my home and hometown. I waited until they could see me no more to wipe the tears blurring my sight.

I walked back into my dorm and started a conversation with the boys nearby. I was an extrovert. People generally liked me on first meeting. It was a gift at most times.

Some of the students were home sick already. I sat with them and spoke encouragingly. I told them that these two years would pass in the blink of an eye and that they would not even notice the years passing by. It was then that I realized that when one was in fear all he had to do is motivate the ones around him and his own fears would vanish.

I was asking everybody about their ambition. Most of them wanted to be doctors. When they posed the same question to me, I said, "I want to get a Nobel prize in whichever field I choose".

Everybody started laughing and made fun of my statement.

I didn't care for it was the truth.

We all then went to the dining hall. After dinner we were all shown a movie by the school management to apparently distract us from being homesick. Not that it worked. But still it was something.

I fell asleep in between though, credits to the slow screenplay.

I was woken up by the other students once the movie got over. I walked straight to my dorm and fell face first on the bed. The street light outside was shining right into my eyes. Yes, I was uncomfortable despite my efforts to choose the best sleeping spot. But even that was not enough to keep me awake as I drifted into sleep.

CHAPTER TWO

ON YOUR MARK

My alarm went off at 6 AM.. I was wide awake due to the excitement and anxiety of my first day in school away from home. I dragged myself to the wash basin to brush my teeth. There was a long queue ahead of me. I decided to shower first, only to find an even longer queue there.

'This isn't going to work. I need to get up earlier tomorrow' I made a mental note.

I looked around and saw that the entire floor had just 20 bathrooms. That was the number of toilets the management had provided for all the hundred or even more students who were going to stay in that floor for the next several months. This was going to take some getting used to.

I waited a long time before it was my turn to get cleaned up. Each bathroom had a bucket and a small slab near the tap for holding our toiletries. The tap dispensed water at a very slow rate. I realised that I couldn't bath within a short time. I brushed my teeth quickly and came out.

I wore my new uniform and stepped out on to the corridor to see about six to seven hundred similarly dressed students standing in a line. I felt I was at the starting line of a marathon. I could already feel the rat race beginning.

We were basically classified into three - Biology, Computer Science, Tamil - according to our 10th grade scores.

Class EB1 - >470 marks

Class EB2- >460 marks

Class EB3 >440 marks

So, EB1-5 stood for biology.

EC1-5 stood for Computer science

TB for Tamil medium and so on.

Girls had a similar classifications like GB7, GC7.

The bar had already been set high. I could feel the pressure building. The heat was on.

I was thinking of all the students in all the schools across the state. So many young people striving towards the same goal.

I walked dejected into EB3 with 448 marks. It didn't feel fair being segregated according to our marks. It wasn't nice to start of with such an inferiority complex though.

As soon as the doors opened, most of my fellow classmates rushed in, pushing each other to secure the seats in the first row while I rushed in to secure the last row corner seat. The rest of the students filed in slowly, filling the rest of the seats.

I wasn't a very a good listener. In fact, I wasn't a listener at all. I always start day dreaming as soon as the teachers started teaching. I had many bad experiences when it came to listening. There had never been a teacher who hadn't shouted at me for drifting off in the middle of a class sitting in the front or middle rows. I wanted the teachers who were going to teach this year to have the worst expectations regarding me. It was better that way.

My class teacher came in and introduced himself.

"Good morning boys. I am Palanivel. I am the class teacher for you. I teach Physics. The rest of your staff will introduce themselves to you as the day proceeds. So now... I want all of you to introduce yourselves with your name, hometown and the reason for joining this school," he said.

As each of them introduced themselves, my heart started beating faster. My mind was going into a frenzy. I really did not want to answer that last question. *Why had I joined this school?* I didn't have a proper answer. I didn't want to answer. Everybody kept saying that they wanted to become a doctor. *' I can say that I am here to get good marks'* I thought to myself.

Before long, my turn came. I stood up and said " I am Shreedher Priyan. I am from Thanjavur". I gave a smile in the general direction of the class and sat down. I breathed in relief and was looking down at my clasped hands. I heard the teacher calling out my name.

"Why did you choose this school though ?"

I froze. This was new to me. I stood quietly few seconds and started stammering, flashes of my past coming to mind.

CHAPTER THREE

Playground Breeze

Don Bosco Higher Secondary School,
Thanjavur.
2005

I stood in awe amazed by the size of the playground in this school. I felt the hot air ruffled my hair. My heart was pounding in excitement. *This was where I wanted to be.* In this school, with its magnificient ground. I watched the football team practicing strenuously. This was the first time that I had seen such a big playground in a school.

My dad was searching for the administrative office to know about the admission procedures. My mom wasn't enthusiastic about me joining the school. "This school is not what you think *thambi*. There is cut throat competition in the society today. You won't understand the implications until its too late. But I won't stop you from joining this place. You'll learn everything in due time".

I was excited. Both my parents had accepted my entry into this school.

I was leaving Maxwell Matriculation Higher Secondary School, my school since childhood. It was known for enforcing discipline besides academics in our district, while Don Bosco School was well known for its involvement in sports and unruly behaviour of some of its students.

I was in my 5th grade . I had a certain level of clarity about what I wanted from my life even back then.

It so happened that on my first day of my new school my father was out of station and my mother was sick.

I opted to go on my own, despite my mother asking me to take a leave of absence. I was looking forward to this new academic year. I was sent in an autorickshaw so that my mom could relax.

The driver dropped me outside the school. I stood at the gates taking a good look at the entire campus. I went to the security and asked "*Anna*, may I know where the fifth standard classroom is? "

"Walk straight, take the first left and you'll be at the primary school block".

I followed his directions and reached there. The whole campus was very confusing with so many buildings. It was different from my old school which had only one block. I asked around and was instructed to find the class in the third floor. I ran upstairs only to find that the classrooms had been shifted to the higher secondary block.

My day had not started off as great as I wanted it. Just as I reached the higher secondary block, the school bell rang and the students started assembling for the daily school prayer.

I made it to my class room in the second floor of the higher secondary block only to find it empty.

'Of course, all students must be at the prayer'. I cursed and walked out of the class room and ran into a teacher.

"What are you doing here?" he asked me.

"I don't know how to get to the school prayer sir. "

"Oh, are you a new admission? " he asked.

"Yes sir".

"It's in the primary block. Now run along."

I ran to the primary block and saw the crowd standing on the ground opposite to the building I was in. Now, the next task was to find the 5th grade students.

'*This is so tedious*', I thought to myself.

I was out of breath. The ropes of my school bag were already pressing into my shoulders.

I wasn't up for searching something again. I decided to stand in the corner and tried to blend in.

I realised it wasn't working when the PET shouted at me for slouching in the corner.

"What do you think of yourself? Don't you have the sense to stand in the appropriate line? "

"I am sorry sir. I don't know in which line the fifth grade students are lined up". So, he seems to be the new admission child, he decided.

I nodded with the sigh of relief. I was tired of answering the same question over and over.

I joined the line he pointed out and started moving my lips like an idiot. The students around me were looking at me like I was an alien.

Students usually shift schools during their entry into higher secondary and here I was transferring one year earlier.

A female PET came and randomly chose students and asked them to stand in a separate line. I didn't know what was happening. I knew I just didn't want to be picked. I didn't want trouble on the first day of school. The teacher stood before me and scanned me from head to foot and asked me to join them. I started to panic. I joined the line and asked,

"Why are we in this line? "

"We are shortlisted to become the patrol leaders" the boy in front of me answered.

"Now, what is a patrol leader?"

"We are supposed to check if the hair, nails, shoes and the uniform of the students are upto the standards set for the primary school level,they will also give a shirt batch to us ," he said

The six of us were asked to stand on the podium out of which four would be chosen. Just like that my day had taken a turn for the better.

As they were about to start the process, a girl from the line shouted out loud,

"Ma‘am you can’t choose him. He’s a new student."

I felt anger boiling inside me. This wasn’t fair. She spoiled one good thing that was supposed to happen to me.

"Are you a new student?" asked the teacher.

" Yes ma’am. "

"Step down from the line," she ordered.

I got down dejected.

The prayer got over in the next fifteen minutes.

I made my way to the class with my school bag after the prayer.

"Why are you late?" the teacher asked me as soon as I entered.

I narrated the whole story and told them that I was a new student before they could ask me.

The teacher then asked all the new students to introduce themselves.

When my turn came, I jumped up and introduced myself with great enthusiasm " I am Shreedher Priyan. I have got transferred from Maxwell School. I shifted from there after seeing that this school has a huge playground and all I want to do is play".

Namakkal.
2010

I was reliving the memories from six years ago and I finally knew what to answer.

"I came to this school because I heard this school won't allow us to play, " I said controlling my tears.

The whole classroom burst into a peel of laughter, including the teacher.

"Is this really why you came here? Are you that hatred with sports?" he asked. I nodded in affirmation.

So, here I stood, six years later, from a kid who had changed schools because it had a playground to a person who had changed school which won't allow students to play.

CHAPTER FOUR

TRAPPED

Namakkal.
2010

The classes went on relentlessly and the teachers pounded volumes of information into our brains.

I felt trapped.

I felt like an animal shut inside a cage without any means of escape.

My previous school operated from 8 AM to 4 PM . But here, I had classes till 7 PM . Even recess was strictly controlled. Ten minutes of recess was given, during which we all had to form a queue to use the restroom and come right back to class.

I remembered all the fun we had during recess in my old school; running around in the playground, meeting our friends from other classes, the jokes shared in the corridor corners and imitating teachers. I missed all of that. This whole set up irked me.

This wasn't how a school should be. It felt like an open prison. If we didn't have the rights to roam around during a simple break of a few minutes, then what else do we have? This was inhuman and infuriating.

I was tall and lanky. The desks in my class were too short. I didn't fit into them. I had to squeeze in and stay in an awkward and uncomfortable position all day long. Those desks were fit only for a primary school kid. But then, one can only expect so much from a school that micromanages all our activities, including the things we did during recess.

I had finished the Physics, Maths, Chemistry, Botany and Tamil subject periods before lunch.

All the studying had rendered me so comically hungry, that I saw chicken legs floating everywhere.

As soon as I heard the bell signaling lunch, I ran to the mess as fast as my famished body would take me and grabbed a plate. I looked in front of me and saw about a hundred students were already standing in front of me in a serpentine queue.

When it was my turn, I got an enormous quantity of rice and sambhar and wolfed it down.

My hunger wasn't satiated and I took another helping of rice and asked for curd. They said they didn't have curd for lunch and instead they offered me buttermilk. I used to fight with my mom over this at home. Now it looked like I didn't have any choice.

Satisfied with the over-dose of food, I went back to attend the afternoon classes. I had a fitful sleep and had no idea what happened in the class. The bell rang at 4 PM breaking for tea and *channa*.

"Today's classes are done at 4 PM as it is the first day. Report for class at 8 AM as usual tomorrow. Class tests will be conducted from 4 to 5.30 PM everyday. Classes will resume and end at 7 PM in the evening" came a circular, which an office attender read out loud to us.

Everybody started cheering. I went back to my room and had a nap. When I finally woke up, it was 8 PM. I looked outside and saw a huge crowd in the mess hall.

'I am late again', I cursed and rushed to get a plate.

"What's on the menu?" I asked one of the students in front of me.

" *Chappathi* and *kurma*" he said.

I loved *chappathis* and these were the best I had tasted. They were limited to four per person and then we could have the rice and curd.

At last, it was bed time. I had had enough for one day. I went back to my dorm and started chatting with my room mates.

Something was different about them.

Then I realised they were in EB1 and EB2 and I was the only one in EB3. The school was sowing superiority in some and inferiority in most of our minds from the very first day.

The first two classes had toppers. The last two had the fun loving and laid back guys. And we, those in EB3, were stuck in the middle, always trying to show that we were good enough.

Only a few students belonging to EB1 and EB2 talked irrespective of the segregation. The attitude that the others had was very demeaning. Based on our quarterly and halfyearly exams they will shuffle the class of students again so I vowed to get better marks so that during re-shuffling I would end up in the first two classes. I wanted to get a good night's sleep before I was ready for the next day's horrors. As soon as the lights went out, I went under the covers and fell into a dreamless sleep.

CHAPTER FIVE

WHERE DID IT ALL START ?

Namakkal.
2010

Next day, my alarm went off at 5 a.m. I got ready for school and had breakfast on time. My class teacher came a few minutes before the bell.

I loved his little talks as he spoke on a lot of philosophical topics. He said all the big things started from a very little spark and it reminded me of a small incident from my childhood because of which now I am sitting here.

Thanjavur.
Sep 25 2002,
One Wednesday

I was in my second grade at that time. I was sick and had taken a day off from school. My mom was a school teacher and dad was a Professor of Chemistry. So they left me in our home and went to work. I took the medicines and had a great time watching Cartoon Network.

I had my lunch around 2 p.m. Suddenly, my dad came in a hurry and got the television remote from me. He changed to a sports channel. I got irritated because I loved watching the *Tom and Jerry* on the screen. He interupted the show mid way. So I went to bed. He called me back and taught me about cricket game. Little did I know that this small incident would be the turning point of my whole life.

That was no ordinary day in the history of Indian cricket. It was the semi finals of the 2002 ICC Cricket Trophy. India was playing against South Africa at Colombo.

My father explained everything about cricket. The men in blue jerseys were playing for India and the men in the green ones were representing South Africa. He then patiently explained the other important rules such as the boundaries, runs, and how a player could get Out. I wondered how a ball would cross such a great length in air for six runs.

My dad was a big fan of Ganguly. *Dada*, as Ganguly was fondly called by his fans, got out at the very beginning of the innings. My dad got tensed but Sehwag was hitting boundaries all over the ground and I started to enjoy those boundaries.

VVS Lakshman got out at the other end and was soon followed by Sehwag.

Rahul Dravid entered the crease. In a short while, Sachin Tendulkar got run out. My father was enraged at the dismal performance of his favourite team. The scoreboard read 4 wickets for 135 runs at the end of 25 overs. My father was shocked after the loss of Sachin's wicket. It was at that time I understood the importance of Sachin's place in the team. My dad's face started to dull down after Sachin returned to the dressing room.

A 20 years old Indian came to bat. After seeing Sehwag hitting those balls so hard, I was very much impressed by this young guy's aggressive batting in the middle order. I did not know the name of the shot that time. Later I learnt it was the 'Pull Shot' which the newcomer was playing well. After playing one such pull shot, he saw the eyes of the bowler with an aggression. Unknowingly I got goosebumps from that look. On that day, I decided I wanted to be a cricket player like him. Having scored 62 runs with 6 boundaries, he got out and he guided India to a decent score of 261.

As soon as India started bowling, Zaheer Khan delivered a full length ball which was smashed by Greame Smith into point region. Again that 20 years old man flew into the air ending in a great dive with the ball in his hand. It was a superhuman catch. I was jumping and shouting in joy with my father. When they were replaying that marvelous catch, I said to my father that he was a player like whom I was going to be in the future. He too appreciated the young player and it felt as if he was appreciating me .

Then the next two South African batsmen named Gibbs and Kallis started destroying our Indian bowlers. They each scored fifty runs and the match started to drift towards the South African side. The Indian fans, both in and out of the stadium, started to lose hope. My dad and I hoped for Ganguly to create some magic or a divine miracle to happen.

Gibbs scored a century and there were wild cheers from the South African fans. When he was at 116 runs and South African score was 1 wicket for 192 at the end of 37 overs, he got injured and got retired hurt. It was the miracle which we were all expecting. The target was 70 runs to be scored from 78 balls for the Proteas.

Harbajan Singh bowled to Jonty Rhodes who had arrived next to the crease. He swept it into fine leg and once again my hero flew from no where to the ball and caught it. They later calculated it and found it was one of the longest dive catch in the world. Two important breakthroughs happened in the match and both were from my hero. He was on fire in the fielding department and changed the whole match single handedly. The two wickets which he dismissed by those two unbelievable catches made a significant change at the end.

South Africa lost their second wicket and from there on they started to lose their wickets. The momentum shifted to the Indian side totally. South Africa lost the match by ten runs.

That day taught me many things in my life - what sports was all about, what cricket was all about and mainly about my father. All of that happened only because he saw the match till the very end. Whether India was going to win or not, he had the mindset to accept both which taught me about belief. Throughout the match, during the batting as well as the bowling sessions, India had no chance of winning this match, yet the team did it.

Now a days, I am seeing lot of people who switch off the TV when there is a small chance of our team loosing. My dad believed that India would win till the last ball of the match with hope. Though this may look like a small incident, it taught me many things.

After the match I wrote my hero's name in my rough note . His name was YUVRAJ SINGH, Jersey number - 12

He was my inspiration, my favorite player, my happiness. In short, *everything.* My ambition was to become a cricket player like him.

**Namakkal,
2010**

I returned from my day dreaming to the class. I later realized how that little spark went on to change a lot of things in my life.

All around me I found guys studious and spending all their time worried about their academic performance. I, on the other hand, was still dreaming about things that happened a long time ago. I didn't know if they had any interest in cricket like I did. I was afraid that I would disturb them if I talked anything other than studies. I was afraid of not being good at studies even after coming to a school like this dedicated only for academics. I knew I was a quick learner. It was time I started making studies as my only priority.

Some situations failed me to become a cricketer but even then I waited eagerly for my hero's performance in the 2011 Cricket World Cup.

CHAPTER SIX

SPARK

Namakkal.
2010

Lunch time. I got my rice and buttermilk along with a house fly in it. Obviously, the entire plate of food ought to be thrown to the dustbin. Again, I went to get some rice and buttermilk, and shockingly it had a house fly again in it. I got an extreme irritation after seeing it. I was in my hungry mode. For a few minutes I was just sitting with the plate as I really did not want to share my food with house fly. It looked like a demon that had come to take away my food. Even then I decided to be gentle with it. I took the house fly and kept it aside on the table. I started to eat.

I went to the afternoon class which was followed by a class test in the evening. I was in shock as everyone started to write for pages. I was writing just one line answers for all the questions and I returned the paper for namesake, thinking that they would not assess these daily tests. Every evening from 4.30 to 5.30 PM we had these class tests and that was the most horrible part of the day in my life I would say. I couldn't even sleep, I wasn't even able to sit in one place, glancing at my watch every few seconds with an urge to know when it would get over.

My world was rotating ten times slower. After the class test, I was in my own sweet world while my friends were listening to the topics taught in the evening class with utmost attention. Each and every word that the teacher said was making me feel guilty of being the only student who was not listening to him.

At the end of class, I was tired and exhausted. Going to the mess would drain what a little energy was left in me. “This is my regular way of breaking my tiredness”, said my room – mate with a sign of facetious expression and convinced me too that I would get used to evening classes as the days went by. It was the most boring day of my life.

All of a sudden, the school chairman called us for a meeting. I was little puzzled as to what it was going to be about. Our school had five directors. Mr. Saravanan was the founder of my school. I had heard some teachers telling that he was a good orator. The other important person among the five was Mr. Mohan as he controlled the functioning of all the hostels.

"Good evening everyone”, he greeted with delight. He then added that most of the old students knew him. ”I am Saravanan, Chemistry teacher and founder of this school”. “I called all you people to tell why we are here, because most of you may feel a little uncomfortable to leave your home and to stay and study here”. I felt a little happy, as he was voicing out my thoughts about this place. “I want you students to fix up your mindsets that, the next two years are going to be the worst time of your life”. I was stunned to hear this statement, because I had an opinion that this man had a positive vibe and now to see him throw around such negative words, left me in great shock.

He continued, "But I wanted to tell one thing. Before you look up to any famous person in this world to be your role model, understand they would have had faced a lot of struggles in their life too.

"They would have worked very hard in their early part of life, and so their economic standards would have improved very much and their sons and daughters will be enjoying that because of them". Now, there was a little shift in his speech. "Most of you have come here to achieve, to do something big in your life". "Note, this brave decision is definitely going to change your life, because residential schooling is not about marks and grades. *It is about sculpting your character*. You have to take care of yourself, as no one except you can decide what is good for your own self.

"It is very difficult to stay away from your home at this time, so completion of two years of residential schooling will be the first greatest achievement here". I felt a little boosted up after hearing these words.

He then registered something strong in our minds. "These two years are crucial in your life. You will be given full freedom to dream whatever you want to become. Once you decide to dedicate these two years for your studies nothing else can deviate you from achieving your dream".

As I had already told you, I was a bad listener and to my wonder, this man had my undivided attention. I went to my bed highly motivated and started to dream even more for the first time.

CHAPTER SEVEN

PASSION

Namakkal,
2010

The next morning, as usual I started lamenting that I had never seen the time-table. Students were excited because of the PET period. Those periods felt heavenly for everyone but unfortunately it was a weekly once period for the first three months in the span of two years. Everyone was excited. They were planning for cricket and football matches. My undying interest would be always for cricket.

I chose football because I didn't want to hit the cricket ball again. I knew it would definitely break my control over it. My house players asked me to be the goal keeper. I was an abecedarian in this sport. It was the long awaited PET period. I envisioned myself as the proud lion in the mid ground.

The school ground was pretty decent than I imagined it would be. We were split into two teams for cricket and football.

I stood as a goal keeper and the game started. Unfortunately, a poor game was being played, and all my team mates ran behind the ball like the mesmerized rats which followed the Pied Piper in the children's story. The ball never crossed the half court and as a goal keeper, I wasn't able to figure out where the ball was. The opponent hit a goal and I couldn't save it because I was not well versed at goal keeping. I asked, "Can I play as the center forward?" They shouted at me with a frown and to my dismay, the opposite team scored another goal. I could not concentrate anymore, as my mind was drifting to the cricket match that was happening on the other side of the ground. One of the ball was hit hard by the batsmen and the ball was slowly rolling towards me.........It was asking me to take and play cricket......................

Don Bosco School,
Thanjavur.
2005

We had two PET periods each week, Wednesday and Friday for grade five, section C children. We were eagerly waiting for the wonderful Wednesdays and fabulous Fridays to come. We were put into different houses Bosco, Savio, Ruva and Thomas. I belonged to the Savio house.

Every PET period, an aggressive football match would take place between the houses, but the problem was that they played only Football. No one wished to play Cricket. So I had no other choice and had to play football like the rest. I was good at sprinting and aggressive attacks on the other team's goalpost. I scored a few goals single-handedly while playing at the center forward position. I became an important player in my class. It was my dream to be the player which was desired by every team. I realized all my inner love for sports and it showed in the way I played. So before learning cricket, I learnt the rules of football and I was a kind of stern player. But still my love for cricket never faded. All on a sudden, I came to know that cricket matches were played during lunch hours on a regular basis by a few students. This excited me as I was longing for one such thing.

I was puzzled as to how to introduce myself to the cricket team which had guys from other classes too. Meanwhile, a ball reached me from the cricket ground. Now the ball was in my court. I picked the chance to approach them. I said, "I am Shreedher, and I would like to join you people". One of the fielders said, "Today the second innings is going on. Let's see for tomorrow, now first throw back the ball". I was overwhelmed with joy.

That day, I went to my house excited. I asked my father to bowl a few balls for me and asked him to bat as I bowled. It was my father who taught me to bat and bowl. So I wanted to show them how much I have learnt to play the sport. I practiced in the play ground nearby with my dad for my first match was the next day. The bat and the stumps we used that day actually came as free compliments for the milk supplement *Milo.*

The next day, a ten overs match started. An inning was played every day and my team chose to field first. I went to my fielding position. Our team was bowling well. The other team scored fifteen runs for four overs and at that particular time, I was thinking about the stumps because they played without proper stumps. It was a volleyball post with a line marked as a stump. It needed more accuracy to hit that mark. When the fifth bowler started to bowl, the opposite team warned our bowler for bending his hand while bowling. The next delivery he automatically bent his hand and my Captain asked me to bowl the remaining five deliveries. This was the first chance that I had got. I was scanning the pitch length. It was smaller than I used to play.

I started my run-up, concentrating on that volleyball post and the shoes of the batsman. I bowled it and in my follow through watched the ball going with an angle towards the volleyball post and the batsmam missed the ball with his bat swung.

TINGGGGGGG!

The ball hit the volleyball post felt heavenly and I could never forget it in my lifetime. Everyone started to shout in happiness and started hugging me from all sides. From that day onwards, I gained the confidence that enough practice and belief in my skill would yield me the fruits of success. That one delivery made me famous in all the sections of fifth grade. After that, everyday we started playing and I scored many runs. Every day I waited for the lunch period and dreamt during the whole day about the game next day. To my wonder, I even started hating Sundays.

During my sixth grade days, I had a close pal named Karthik Narayanan, a forward caste boy.

The reason that I am mentioning his caste was because some of my other friends who belonged to the same caste never allowed me to step inside their houses. I never understood the meaning of untouchability at that time. I got to know the concept of untouchability through an incident. Long ago, we used to usually play in a ground near our school. On that day some other school boys occupied it and we took another ground. To our disappointment, we found some boys playing there already. One of my friend asked them to bowl some balls since we didn't have much time to play a whole match. After him it was my turn to bat. Then I asked those boys to bat so that I can bowl. My friend yelled at me that there was no need for them to bat. I looked at him in confusion. He came near me and whispered that they were untouchables.

I was taken a back by his statement. It was not because of his choice of words but due to the intent behind them. I didn't know the meaning of untouchability then but what I did know was that it was rude and against the spirit of sports to quit in the middle of a game. Those guys had bowled for me to bat and it was only right for me to bowl so they can bat. I argued with my friend about this and left only after bowling a good number of overs.

In complete contrast, Karthik was an easy-going person. He didn't tolerate when such biased comments were passed in his presence. We became closer with time and learnt many new skills like playing musical instruments. Kartik's father was a cricket player and hence Karthik knew a lot about the nuances of the game. I used to go to his house and within the compound, we played many interesting matches. He taught me lots of techniques in bowling - like holding the ball along the stitches, how to release the ball and how to swing it. After lots of practice, I learnt to be a better bowler than most of them.

Namakal.
2010

After 5 years, the cricket ball had come to me again, like calling me for a rough and tough match, though the player from the opposite football team came dribbling aggressively towards me. I signalled to the one remaining player in the defensive position to come near the goal post. He looked at me puzzled.

I ran to take the cricket ball. All my football mates shouted at me to guard the posts. I threw the ball to those cricket players standing afar and started to sprint towards the football guy moving towards my team's goalpost. As usual, my aggression busted out. I pushed the opposite team guy with my shoulder to take possession of the ball. It was technically allowed in a football game. I got the ball from him and the football was spinning under my foot . Everyone in my team started calling me to pass the ball to them. I ignored their voices and started sprinting to the left side of the court. I tried to cross some players and no one managed to catch me while I ran.

For the first time, the ball had crossed to the half side of the other team. Within a span of 10 seconds, I had reached the other goal post. I took a shot which unfortunately went above the crossbar. I looked with the eyes of a proud sportsman at all those who had been shouting at me since the match began. The PET teacher blew the whistle signaling the end of sports time. *The day was mine.*

CHAPTER EIGHT

STRANGER FRIEND

Namakkal.
2010

Fate always played a very active and vital role in the lives of a few. One such instance was with the little children who were sent to hostel for studies. This was really a sad thing. My heart exploded when thinking about their lives.

Don't they deserve happiness? Don't they deserve some family time? I couldn't bear to see them living such a caged life. All this was because of their overconcerned educated parents. Thinking that studies is the only major criterion for one's survival in this world. They never thought about the mental and emotional turmoil they were putting their own loved ones through. The irony was that these kids never knew that they have been caged.

To my knowledge, these kids needed to be in a family to know what life actually was. As far as I was concerned, life was actually about getting sent to grandparents house during school vacations, playing games,visiting relatives during holidays, being with friends and enjoying festivals.

This would really bring a big change in one's life. A child would never know how to tackle a family situation unless they know what a family was all about.

One day after having my breakfast earlier, my friend asked me to wait for him outside the mess hall. I was sitting on the cement floor. In the school campus there were a couple of stray dogs. One of them sat near me and was looking at my face with hunger in its eyes.

I patted its forehead and I knew that although stray dogs did not get proper food, they yearned for the love and warmth of people. Since I had reared a street dog named "Rocky" when I was young, I naturally cared about this one too. I am a big fan of the Rocky movies that starred Sylvester Stallone as the iconic boxer. Although there were many great lines in those movies, one dialogue endeared to me the most-

'It isn't about how hard you hit, its about how hard you get hit and keep moving forward '.

My father considered keeping the dogs inside the house was wrong as it restricts their freedom. He also believed that tying them up with a chain and restricting their sex life was equivalent to earning a bad karma for human beings. So we left our "Rocky" free outside our home. We fed it every time and, at night we locked him inside our compound.

At one point of time, Rocky started harming all the passers-by. Everyone in our neighbourhood started to accuse us for its deeds. We were confused as to what we needed to do with Rocky. Many people suggested us to call for the animal control service and give it away. But I knew there weren't many dogs as good and loyal as my Rocky and surely they would kill him.

We didn't want that pathetic incident to happen. So we hired an auto and took him to a safe place. We left him at the outskirts of the town, near a river bank. I was crying the whole way to the river bank. I was numb with an overflowing emotion which I couldn't explain. Rocky ran behind our auto for a while and that was the first heart break I felt in my life.

All of a sudden, this particular memory flashed across my mind. I went to hostel and took some biscuits to feed the stray dog. I usually did that because of some guilt which had built up inside me unknowingly. We became friends and I used to share all my feelings with him. Those looking at the scene must have definitely thought that I was a little eccentric. Dogs had a natural tendency to understand words and feelings. Dogs are the best gifts to the human race given by the God.

Like me, there was another person who was very close to that dog. I wondered who he was. When I enquired about him to my friends, it was Mr. Suresh Babu, the Zoology teacher for the higher classes. He stayed in our hostel. He was the best tutor and a favourite amongst the students .

Many used to appreciate his style of teaching. Once I went to the higher secondary block to just observe his class. I stood outside the class to listen how good his teaching was. He had a rough and manly voice which was so loud that the teachers next door couldn't take class.

Apparently, his commanding voice and his great teaching skills just prevailed as a role model for many and a nuisance to a few. Those were the times, I felt jealous of the class toppers because Babu sir taught only their class.

Whereas we had a Maths teacher who always switched off the fan while teaching because his voice was not audible to the last benches. If I had been in his place I would talk louder, instead of making my class physically uncomfortable. I initiated and addressed this particular issue to one of the directors but still this continued to happen. This made me build a kind of hatred towards mathematics.

As the days passed with such silly issues, our quarterly examinations were around the corner. All of us started to panic and were preparing sincerely and whole heartedly, including me, because we were informed that these marks would be considered for our class shuffling.

CHAPTER NINE

DAD'S DEAL

Don Bosco School,
Thanjavur
2007

Lot of fights took place between my parents and me with cricket being the point of contention. A day without cricket left me agitated and unhappy. Throughout the day I would be in an off mood if I did not play cricket. Usually they would let me play, but on the days of exam I would be stopped from stepping out fearing that, this would affect my scores. Later, I developed a habit of writing a letter and leaving it at the doorstep, promising them that I would come back home and study and they allowed me playing cricket .

Also I used to add a P. S. at the end of the letter stating that they shouldn't expect me to come home before 6 p.m. My father understood my love for cricket and that was the reason why fathers remain as the first and life long heroes for many. But my mom used to lock me up inside the house. I would plead with her to let me go outdoors. She started feeling that I was irresponsible with my schoolwork and requested dad to advice me. I felt happy that unlike other fathers, my dad took the point of advising me in a motivating manner and promised to enroll me in the district cricket association if I scored well. I took up his challenge seriously and used it as a motivating factor to take my preparation for the upcoming exams seriously . I studied continuously for ten days without even resting and scored the first rank in my class.

As I had kept my word, my dad honored the deal. He took me to the Sathya Stadium in Thanjavur, which was 8 kilometers from my house. There I observed all the players practicing every other sport except cricket. We went there in the evening and waited for a while. At 5 p.m, three seniors came rolling the cricket mat which was worn out and a stinky kit. They started their practice.

My dad asked them, " May I know, where is the coach?"

They replied, "He will come after two days,".

We left the place with the hope of meeting him after two days. My dad requested the coach to enroll me in the district association. The coach gave a weird and disrespectful look. In my view everyone in the world created by God had to be treated with respect. My dad was a Chemistry professor, even if my dad was not a teacher he should be treated with respect simply because of one strong reason - HE WAS MY DAD, AND HE HAD COME ALL THIS WAY FOR ME. This particular attitude just disturbed my mind badly that I lost any respect I had for that man as a coach. I happily went to practice for two days and I felt bored, because one person had to bat, three others had to bowl and the rest had to do fielding. There were no proper nets and no proper cricket balls. One thing I learnt was that the difference between a cricket ball and a Cosco tennis ball. I was little afraid to field because the cricket ball would hurt if you got hit and the saddest thing was there were no one to teach the proper techniques. So I decided to quit and learn by myself.

I started playing in the street again. It was then that I thought of forming a team with all the guys from my school who were enthusiastic about cricket but not properly trained. When I requested my PE teacher about this, he convinced me about the importance of other sports in that particular school. He also insisted that there would be a few problems – the so called "politics in sports" . He convinced and made me join the hockey team. He also made me buy the necessary kit and I played hockey as a part of the school team for several months.

I missed the rush of hitting big sixes and bowling high speed deliveries in cricket.Therefore with a fickle mind I left the hockey team. One of my friends said that a sport in any school will always depend on successful players it had. When Don Bosco school was started here, students would have got their first victories in Football and Hockey which continued to this day.

Namakkal.
2010

I had joined a residential school primarily to get away from this cricket addiction. But I had a lot of nervous energy which I could not spend on playing cricket. I used to punch the walls and shake my legs to relieve the energy. Since they were destructive to my body, I then distracted myself by daydreaming about all the things that I would buy and do after I joined a good college – riding a Pulsar bike, buying my first Honda Civic car, going on a world tour and several others.

CHAPTER TEN

PONDER

Thanjavur,
2007.

Every Indian cricket fan including our Don Bosco cricket gang in which Arun, my team mate, was waiting for the ICC ODI World Cup. We used to watch matches together as our houses were nearby.

The Indian team was not in its best form. I used to wait for Yuvraj Singh's performance. He was a stylish player who was in vogue at that time. Unfortunately, the team failed in the group stage itself.

People started to hate the Indian team for giving such a poor performance. They started burning effigies of the star players to show their displeasure. I was irritated with this behaviour of the 'fans'. I felt this kind of attitude really won't show the love for the players and would't help the morale of the players in any way. They always wanted India to win and they were not ready to accept defeat.

The T20 world cup was just around the corner and Mahindra Singh Dhoni was the captain of the young team. It was my hero Yuvraj Singh's turn to shine in South Africa. He was in a verve to win the matches as he had lost the chance to lift the ODI World Cup previously.

He showed his true potential against England by hitting fifty runs in twelve balls – a record unbroken to this day. Even after fifteen years, it was a delight to watch the six consecutive sixes he smashed on that day in front a packed stadium. It was all the more special since it was the English pacer Andrew Flintoff who had triggered Yuvraj before that fateful over with his sledging.

In the semi finals, when India was struggling with Australia's bowling, it was Yuvraj who came to the rescue. He flicked Bret Lee's ball into a monstrous six which travelled well over hundred and nineteen meters. He got a massive score of seventy from thirty balls that turned the winds of victory towards India.

Finally India won the world Cup in an epic nailbiting thriller of a final against its arch rival Pakistan. Yuvraj Singh grabbed the 'Man of the Series' title.

I was on cloud nine that day. Every ball that Yuvraj hit in that tournament was etched in my memory. What a stylish player he was! No one could hit a perfect flick shot like him.

After watching Yuvi's sixes, I badly wanted to make cricket as my career. It became my dream. One fine day, Arun's father came to meet my father regarding change of our school from Don Bosco to Kendriya Vidhyalaya - a Central government school situated inside the Air force station. They felt that CBSE syllabus would get us into prestigious institutions like IIT and NIT when compared to state board syllabus.

Lot of heated discussions happened regarding this. I said a strong no to KV school since I was happy with my current school.

After few days, I came to know that we would be the first batch in KV school. A new school with students from eight grade and below. All of a sudden, the words of my friend spoken a long ago flashed in my mind's eye – 'Any sport in a school depends on the first batch forerunners'. I thought why I had to to play hockey in Don Bosco School when it was better to move to a new school to start the trend of playing cricket there.

Thus, I decided to join Kendriya Vidhyalaya School. I got to know that we had to pass an entrance test to join the school. There would be only one section for each class of thirty five and it was very tough to get an admission there. Since I knew the competition I was facing , I decided to prepare well for the entrance examination.

The biggest problem I had at that time was the Hindi language. Invariably, all the students getting admitted there should be fluent in Hindi because Tamil was not in option in that KV school curriculum. Apparently, I had to prepare for an exam in Hindi. So I went for Hindi tuition for two months to clear the entrance exam.

The D-day arrived and I wrote the entrance exam. To everyone's surprise, I got selected there. I was overwhelmed that I had cracked a tough exam in my first attempt with a good score. After entering, I came to know that, the Kendriya Vidhyalaya schools were started for the children of Central government employees, mainly in the Indian Armed Forces. Since there were lot of transfers during their tenure, Central government employees' children were given the first priority and then came the state government employees' children. I was selected not only because of my entrance marks, but also as my dad was a state government employee. A class of thirty five with fifteen other state people and twenty Tamilians.

CHAPTER ELEVEN

FIRST BLUSH

Namakkal.
2010

We all were getting ready for the next 2011 World cup and we used to share our ideas on which players will make it to the playing XI of the Indian squad. We had finalized our dream team before the BCCI and all our predictions were true. I was still worried because Yuvi was not in his prime form before this world cup. It was a nerve wracking wait to see whether the selectors would choose him. To my pleasure, the members added him to the squad which started some controversies.

We waited eagerly for the 2011 world cup, and were disappointed when the school management decided not to allow students to watch those matches. Instead we would be spending the time for our study hours. *Wonderful!*

It was the that time of the year when we had our quareterly exams. Everyone started studying as we had been told earlier that these marks would be included for our class shuffling. I got used to the regular timings of the school. I was sure that I would ace these tests. Mathematics was giving me a tough time but I could not blame anyone for that. I was not able to maintain my notes properly because, he still kept switching off the fan even after I took up the issue with the principal several times. I didn't have time to take photocopies of my classmate notes too. I was afraid that this would hamper my wish to move to a better section. I managed to understand the concepts in Physics and other subjects and learnt them well. I realized that it took me three to four times longer than the time required for the toppers to grasp a concept. I decided that the only way to beat such high competition was to work trice as hard.

Everyone was serious and proactive. The entire hostel had the ambience of a Himalayan ashram filled with yogis meditating on *Shivratri*. I was the only bloke who took this exam casually and come what may, my bed time was always at ten o'clock. The study time came to an end at eleven o'clock and until then we have to be in the school block. Between 10 p.m. to 11 p.m , I used to loiter around the school to stop myself from dozing off, as our warden would shout like a banshee if he caught us with our eyes shut.

For the first few days I tried to stay awake. It was very tough and I decided to sleep before the rest of the guys with the help of my friends. I slept before the study time ended and when the warden crossed my room, I would put up an award worthy performance with my book in hand.

Finally, the exams got over. Everyone said they had given their best. For the next few days we ditched our textbooks and had some fun. We watched a movie arranged by the school management, chatted late into the night about crushes we had in our previous schools. When it was my turn to tell about my first crush, I blushed in excitement just by the memory of her.

Kendriya Vidhyalaya,
Thanjavur.
2008

The KV school's ambience was fresh and many teachers were not posted. We only had teachers for Social Science and PET. For a month we had five PET classes per day. What else did a student need more than the bliss of not having a regular teacher for a scheduled class? It felt heavenly!

We enjoyed every second of this freedom. Everyday we woke up with 'in the know' mode and this time it was about our Principal Mr. Rajapan, who got transferred from Kerala.

One day before the morning classes started, we went to the ground to play until the prayer started. He was a punctual man who came early and was not hesitant to spank any student who misbehaved. So we always used to maintain a safe distance from him.Usually we never attend school prayer meetings instead we played in school ground .Oneday Principal came and gave enough beatings to our back and sent us to prayer meeting,with irritated mood I went to prayer.

It was then that I noticed her for the first time. Pooja D'Souza, the astoundingly beautiful and graceful North Indian girl, from my class was standing in the prayer group. She had a voice so enchanting and put everyone under a spell. I always had a special craze for girls who could sing classical Indian *Carnatic* music .

I used to skip the prayers regularly. After I saw her in the choir, I started attending the prayer sessions just to hear and admire her singing. Though I was not fluent in speaking neither English nor Hindi, I had a strong confidence in my abilities to communicate about my feelings. How could I when she was constantly surrounded by her friends. To make things worse they always used to talk with each other in Hindi. I was not very fluent in Hindi and this discouraged me from approaching her. Thus I turned jealous when a random guy spoke to her in Hindi. I was getting needlessly possessive over her.

Kiruba, a friend of mine, told me that he was in love with Pooja, which was totally shocking to me. Entire class was supporting him and no one knew that I too had feelings for Pooja.

'*Varanam Ayiram*' was an extraordinary movie .It created a vogue of learning guitar like the hero of that movie,that movie inspired me to learn guitar.

There was a scene in the movie in which the hero confessed his love to the heroine, who he had met for the first time on the train. It was magical to say the least. I must have watched and practiced that particular scene for nearly a hundred times, just to confess my feelings to Pooja in a romantic manner using Hindi *shayaris*.

Kiruba proposed his love to Pooja. She was not interested in reciprocating his love and that made me fly in the sky with joy.

I was waiting for my chance. I became the leader for *Pandiyan* house. Pooja was the leader for *Cheran* house. During the annual school sports day, we had a march past of all the four houses. We used to practice for a few weeks. For practice, we used to go to the ground near Air Force officers quarters which was two kilometers away from our school. While returning from one such practice session, I overheard that Pooja had not reported to the march past practice. She was unwell and had stayed back in the classroom. I thought this was the right chance to express my feelings to her. I felt guilty and awful in my heart as I was making her take a decision when she was vulnerable to illness. I was left without a choice. I knew that I would not get a better opportunity to talk to her alone after this. So I ran to the class with our house flag in my left hand and my lunch kit in the other. In my hurry to get to the class first, my house flag dropped and it hit my shin. I fell down with a big thud.

There was a shooting pain in my wrist and I was rushed to the hospital by my dad. After taking a X-ray scan, the doctor said that I had fractured my right wrist bone. That was how my first attempt of proposing love came to a crashing end. The next day I was not able to attend the sports day as a house captain. This hardly bothered me, but I was upset when the doctors advised me not to stress my wrist for at least six months. Which meant that I was not to play cricket for half a year. I was distraught that I had failed in my first encounter with love and hampered my sports time in the process.

The next year I wanted to be in the same school house in which Pooja was. After requesting with several people, I managed to do it. Pooja and I were the captains of *Cheran* house. This was the time I was planning. I had lot of chances to talk to her about my feelings for her. All those who expressed their feelings to their crushes possessed nerves of steel and a courageous heart.

I always motivated her that we would make our Cheran house the most envied by winning many trophies. We put our best efforts and our house won the overall Championship Trophy. I was awaiting to use this golden opportunity.

As usual, there was a little voice of logic that wanted me to back off, but my mind was bent on doing it on the annual sports day when we would be presented with the trophy. I kept dreaming about the two of us lifting the coveted trophy and I planned to propose my love to her in that special day but life threw a bouncer ball to me. Pooja's father got transferred to Rajasthan. All my dreams of lifting my love along with the trophy just got shattered. Eventually, there were other changes in life that made me to change to a different school.

Namakal.
2010

My friends bombed me with questions relentlessly after listening to my story, " Does she know that you loved her atleast now?"

"Did you ever try contacting her after that?"

My answer was 'No' to most of their questions. I didn't know how to contact her as a lot of things happened in my life at that time. I didn't know her father's phone number or hers. "How was I going to find her?" was the only question that popped in my mind for many days after she left.

One of my friends in Namakkal school suggested a social network site named Orkut and asked me to search her profile on it. It sounded brilliant to me as I was totally unaware about Orkut that time. He explained to me the basics of how to use the website . I started my quest to contact her during my vacations. Unfortunately her name was not there. After trying tirelessly for several months I had to admit defeat. That is the story of how destiny brought an end to my very first love.

CHAPTER TWELVE

HALT

Namakkal.
2010

Exam results came with a bang!

Zoology - 68 /75,
Botany - 65/75,
Physics - 120 / 150 ,
Chemistry - 130 / 150,
Maths-155/200

I had got a decent score in all subjects but it was not good enough to move to a better section in the shuffling process. The Maths score was particularly an eyesore.

The toppers in the other classes had got more than hundred and thirty-five. So the rest of us felt that we couldn't move into their class, and this shattered our self esteem for a while.

Some of my classmates started weeping uncontrollably. Shanmugan, one of my friends , cried like he had lost his entire life. I was trying my best to cheer him up inspite of feeling pity for myself.

"Don't worry dude, we have yet another chance in our forthcoming half-yearly exam".

He wept and made a comment which just shocked me, "You guys can enter into medicine based on your quota. But there is no such chance for a forward caste guy like me and I must secure more marks than you. I need to work really hard."

What he said was not completely untrue. Discrimination based on one's birth was unfair. Therefore, I listened patiently and empathized with him.

Similarly, I consoled many students who had a deep thought that marks were the only parameter to measure success in life. I knew this was a humbug.

There were a lot of things in life other than this and I also understood that these people had never experienced failures. I thought, 'No one in this school would have experienced failures like me.

So I never got down in the dump about my marks'. I started figuring out where I was failing and started to rectify over there. Biology and Chemistry were my strengths but I struggled with Physics and Maths.

From then on, I focused more on Maths. The major challenge that prevailed was my incomplete notes due to the annoying nature of my Math teacher.

So I decided to copy from one of the best students in my class. While copying, I understood where I had gone wrong. It felt like an imposition I gave to myself daily. I also started working on the Physics problems hour of the night. By the time the half-yearly exams arrived, I got a clear-cut idea about how I should perform in the exams to get maximum marks.

The best part of those days was the new Zoology teacher, Suresh Babu sir transferred from EB1 to EB3 section to improve our class Biology scores, who was the reason for my interest in Biology. He used to clear many doubts I had in Zoology when I visited him often.

We became friends over time. Whenever I met him he always encouraged me to look into a Biology magazine that he had. Also, we often discussed many interesting topics in Microbiology.

He was an amazing teacher who kindled my interest in the natural sciences. He was the one who instilled the idea within me to become a Doctor.

"Why don't you aim to be a Doctor" he asked one day.

"My ambition is to become a Nobel laureate, sir!" I exclaimed.

"So what's in that? You can be a Nobel laureate in this field!", he countered.

I was in a fix! I knew that my cut-off score had to be atleast 197.75/200 in Biology to become a doctor. I felt it was impossible for me as I knew I wasn't that smart. Then I felt I was losing buoyancy in my progress.

"Mark my words! If you pass through this rough patch, you will become a great person in this field. I know about you. You are a remarkable guy, which is more than enough to become a good doctor", he praised me.

I didn't know whether I was worthy of such high praise but it felt nice to listen to someone speaking good about me in this tough place.

From that moment on, I considered myself in the medical field and visualized how my parents would be proud of me when I become a specialist. I decided to work towards making that dream a reality and prepared myself to win this long race.

I was way behind many people in this race, yet I had a strong hope and faith in myself. I had decided to take up the challenge and kept running without any halts because I already knew the struggles and the problems that were part of the dream.

I made a plan and set a short goal to score high in the half-yearly exams to enter the second topper's class. I had already lost the chance to become a cricketer. I was not going to let my ambition of becoming a doctor meet a similar fate.

CHAPTER THIRTEEN

EFFORTS

Namakkal,
2011

One fine morning they asked us to gather in the ground to change our rooms in the hostel. We got ready and sprinted to the ground. When I heard my room number was 201, I rushed to enter first and took the corner cot for myself. I sat there patiently till everyone entered. Later, I shifted my entire stuff with the help of my new roomie Elancheziyan. The new room gave me positive vibes. Whenever I laid down on my double-decker cot, I wished to have a few motivational lines in my line of sight, and so I wrote a couple of wordswith a marker in my exiting list.

Dr. Shreedher Priyan
Yuvraj Singh.
Nobel Prize for Medicine.
Pooja.
Himalayas - My dreamland to travel.
Guitar – to play like Varnam ayiram Surya

My first quote was '*Everything ends happily, if not then it is not the end*', from *Om Shanthi Om*. The next was '*Nothing is permanent except change'.*

After arranging all my things,and settling down in my new room , I took a new note for Maths to copy everything, I made plans to improve my academic performance over the next few weeks. Every day I took an extra effort to improve my methods of studying.

One day, I was unable to get up from my bed. I felt a burning sensation in my eyes and my temperature was high. I couldn't stand up and so I decided to bunk my morning study hours but my staff in charge forced me to come to school.

I told him that I was tired and could hardly stand. He gave me a paracetamol tablet and insisted that I go to school after my body temperature came down. I requested him to allow me to go home since my bowel was unwell.I rang my father to pick me up from the school. Finally, both my father and mother turned up and took me to Thanjavur. I was advised by the doctor to take a blood test, which revealed that I was affected by Typhoid. The doctor recommended me to take rest for the next seven days and prescribed medicines.

I felt much irritated to stay back for seven days because it distanced me from the positive vibes in my new room. I thought that every effort of mine had gone down the drain. I was worried that my exam marks would be affected because of this illness. I wished to study but I couldn't, this similar situation had happened to me in 2008.

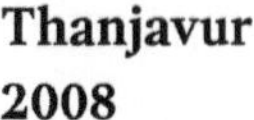

Thanjavur
2008

I had suffered a wrist fracture during my 8th grade when I

was in KV school. My cast was removed after a few weeks with doctor's advice. Later, I went to a physiotherapist for nearly a month. He advised that I shouldn't stress my injured hand for the next six months. I was grief-stricken that I would not able to play cricket.

After several days, I saw an advertisement for the Under- 14, Thanjavur district cricket team selection at Kittu ground, Thanjavur, which was near my place. Previously it was held at Sathya stadium which was far from my place. All my friends went for the selection and I was unable to attend because of my injury. This frustrated me, so I went to my dad and got permission to watch the selection. I wasn't completely honest with him as I had an idea to participate in it. I didn't want to disclose to him.

I reached the ground, enrolled in the All-rounders list and began my warm-up. It was two months since I had last set foot on the ground. I was unable to bring back my old pace during bowling. There was still a chance for me to get selected as the selection committee observed only the line and length of the bowlers. I bowled slow balls with proper line & length and practised batting by facing a few deliveries without giving heavy work to my wrist. I had pain despite my best efforts to avoid it. Then I took the photocard of Yuvraj Singh from my pocket and prayed to God that I should get selected. My prayers were intense because I had worked many years for this opportunity.

Then the coach came forward to announce the result. It was one of the most awaited moment for me. He called out the names - Arun, Raja, Kiruba, Karthick Balaji. They were all my schoolmates. Next I heard the name - Shreedher Priyan. My name sounded sweeter than ever at that moment. I was ecstatic upon hearing my name. I felt very proud to be one among the thirty member squad, eligible to participate in the Under- 14 Inter-District Tournament, that was going to take place in Coimbatore.

I was on my way home from the ground with the happiest face because of the what I had achieved. I didn't expect that I would perform well with my broken wrist. I was sure that I would seize the opportunity to prove myself even though I was in a worse condition.

I was now worried about how to reveal this to my parents. I was very sure about my mom as she used to beat me from time to time as she felt it was necessary to discipline me. It was simply because she cared a lot about my health during the initial days of my injury. As I expected, I was whacked hard and yelled at by them. Finally, my dad allowed me to attend the tournament, provided the doctor permitted me.

My heart pumped hard on the day of the doctor's review. I held my breath the entire time he was examining the X-ray film and other reports. Fortunately, he said, "The report looks perfect but participating in the tournament is a risk. I won't recommend you to play at this stage but if you really feel this as a window of opportunity then go and grab it". I thanked him and started focusing on the tournament.

I didn't have proper shoes for my regular practice and finding a pair that fit me was always a problem. It was a forever nuisance for me to get the shoe of size 12. Also, it was even harder to get shoes in local shops at Thanjavur. I requested my dad to get me branded shoes that cost around 2000 rupees. Even though it was hard-earned money for him, he agreed to buy them. My dad and I roamed the entire city of Thanjavur in search of branded shoes but we failed to get them. I became restless and so I settled for a shoe despite it being a smaller size. "You have decided to spend so much money, then you should get one that gives you complete satisfaction," said my father.

Finally, we travelled to Trichy to purchase a shoe. Often, I became worn out when I walk with my dad, but he never showed fatigue in his face. Only at that instance, I understood about his will and energy and it provoked me to follow his footsteps. We found the shoe that was perfect for my feet and we returned home happily.

In the next few days, my cricket net practice started successfully. I was admired by everyone for my bowling, except my coach whom I met months back in Sathya stadium. My batting shots were hawkish and impressive. They asked me to get a new bat if I wished to play every day. They suggested that would be the way to become an all-rounder.

On hearing this, I felt guilty because my dad had already spent so much on my shoes. We are not a very wealthy family that time. My dad had to pay our home loan. With this rush of thoughts, my conscience did not allow me to burden him anymore. Therefore, I had decided to give up my wish to become an all-rounder. I told them that I couldn't make the ends meet. Hence I enrolled my name under fast bowlers. They assigned me as the opening blower.

All set for the tournament, it was the time to fill my details in the form. They asked my date of birth, I told them that I was born in July 1994. They shocked me by saying that I was not eligible to play because, the date of birth of the player for the tournament should be after September 1994. After hearing this I rushed home to ask my dad whether we could change my date birth to 26.9.1994 since it was a handwritten form. He was deeply disappointed on hearing this, but still, he didn't approve forthe changing of my date of birth. He thought that it would affect my future opportunities if it was changed. I struggled a lot to come out of it because of missing the great opportunity in two months difference. It was even more hurting when I saw my classmates participating in the tournament.

I was mad about my situation for several days afterwards. Slowly, I learnt to deal with bad luck in my life. That summer I got a chance to participate in a district cricket camp for three weeks. Mr. Venkat, the TNCA appointed coach, very professional cricketer came to train us. We were almost thirty trainees of different age groups.

Every day we practised twice from 5 to 8 a.m and 3 to 7 p.m. Some of our fitness sessions were tough and physically taxing. Our coach made us run four rounds around the ground, after which we jogged and shuttle run for ten times. Most of us were fatigued and I was scratched all over. That was the first time I had expereienced such a terrible workout in my life.

After the hard warm-up, each of us has to take ten flat and high catches. If we did not do them with the proper form then we were instructed to do from the beginning which turned most of our hands red. Slip catches were the most difficult catches as they needed a very good reflex. I realised that this tough one was a cakewalk for me. Slowly with each passing day, I found my abilities. Not only me but also Mr Venkat also identified this and was impressed with my bowling. Since I was under 16, I got the chance to bowl for both under 14 and 19 batsmen. Those were some wonderful days, where I got to bowl twenty overs each day.

One day, my coach found the biggest flaw in my bowling style. He told me if a player was a right-hand bowler, then they use the left leg to jump and right leg to land, while using the left leg to stretch and release the ball. On the contrary, I used the right leg to jump and land. I took his suggestions very seriously and worked on it. This gave me extra pace after I practised it for several times for a few days. I also started using my wrist to generate pace and seam which gave me extra confidence in swinging the ball. My natural bowling action got an in swing on it. It was a double edged sword but I controlled it with my bowling practice.

I had a thought that the great bowler was the one who took the highest number of wickets but this camp proved me wrong. It was because of my coach who made me realize that the best bowler was one who repeated the same style of bowling for the entire over with the accuracy of hitting exact length in the right line and with a perfect pace. He also recommended us to learn the bowling skills by watching the matches of Glen McGrath. At the end of the camp, I felt happy and contented about becoming a professional cricketer.

CHAPTER FOURTEEN

PROCURE

**Namakkal,
2011**

After my days of typhoid fever, I came back to school with a lot of pressure to catch up with the topics that I had missed. My next mission was to succeed in the half-yearly examination. I continued to work very hard. My body also struggled a little bit to withstand the overtime studies but somehow I managed and wrote my half yearly exams with the all strength within me.

My hard work bore fruit. Elanchezian and I topped our class. My scores were 190/200 in Maths, 142/150 in Physics, 145/150 in Chemistry, 73/75 in Botany and 75/75 in Zoology. That was a good score, it paved the way for a lot of changes in my life. I never knew that it would be the happy moment of my life.

I ran with anticipation to meet Suresh Babu sir. He saw my report card and he was very happy with my progress. I started enjoying that moment and I was sure to move to thesecond topper's class in the next shuffling. I felt this was the reward for my sacrifices. I informed my parents about this exciting moment during my weekly phone turn. I still remember the way I spoke to them. Amidst all this, I was lambasted for my high marks in Zoology. Many gossiped that Suresh Babu sir had released the question paper to me, and that he showed favouritism towards me. These comments hurt me deeply because I alone knew the real struggle I faced. After a few days of distress, I forgot this due to the start of the 2011 ICC Cricket World cup tournament.

The sad thing was that we had no opportunity to watch the matches at the hostel. The only option we had was the hostel warden's mobile to know the scores of the match. This was not a practice that was allowed for us but we were unable to stop ourselves from doing that. We used to send a boy to ask for the score and he would circulate the cricket score to the entire hostel otherwise all of us could get dismissed from hostel anytime .

One day I had a huge fight with my classmate because he said Yuvraj Singh was a poor player and so he would not be selected for the tournament and affect India's chances of winning the World Cup if Yuvi got selected. I was enraged on hearing this and started hitting him hard.

This altercation slowly evolved a quarrel between two teams. I wagered that Yuvraj Singh would hit minimum 35 runs in any position he played. This turned out into serious gambling in our hostel, and many started betting on their favourite players. Everyone was very curious about the first match between India and Bangladesh. As I said Yuvraj Singh was in the team, but it was Virat Kohli who became the show stopper of the match.

The second match between India and England was a huge relief for me since my prince hit 58 runs in 50 balls with nine boundaries. I stacked a lot of money in the bet, many questioned seriously about the position of Yuvraj in that World Cup but I was pretty sure that he would always come up with exemplary shots only when he was in utmost pressure. He often surprised his adversaries with unexpected shots.

The next match with Ireland was also captivating because that was the first time in history for an all-rounder to score 5 wickets and 50 runs. Yes, Yuvi bagged up the Man of Match award with this great achievement. From there he maintained his tremendous form. He was once again crowned as the Man of the match with 51 runs and 2 wickets against Netherlands.

I was in high hopes that Yuvi would rock one more time but unfortunately not against South Africa. India had to win the next match with West Indies to enter quarter-finals. This match was something unforgettable because Yuvi was spitting up blood while he was batting in the crease. He did not stop playing, he continued his innings and also scored a century. Most of us who bet on Yuvi in the hostel thought that he was hit by the ball, but none of us knew that was his initial phase of lung cancer. I later wondered how a man could be brave enough in the field after being affected by a deadly disease. He turned out to be a legend at the end of that innings. I just realised his dedication towards his game and nation was the reasons behind his legendary titles.

"The artist who performs for the people will forget himself!
He will cover his tears and give pleasure!
Tigers never cry, even the birds does not know how to cry!
When you enter the battlefield –
you can't feel the thorns stitching your foot
Son ... son.... There is no rest of the air!
Art never fails ! "
- Poet Vairamuthu

The day had come and I was so curious enough to know whether India would beat the three times champion Australia.

Initially, we had many fights amongst us in compering our favourite players but I never showed hatred towards other players. Later the situation was upside down where the hostellers who criticised Yuvraj started admiring him. We became devotees of my favourite player. We all knew that if we won over Australia in this match then we would be the champions for sure. Since the 2003 World Cup final match continued to be in the nightmares of every 90's kid , we were kept at the edge of the seat during every minute of the game. After the top order collapsed, Yuvi single-handedly pushed India in the quarterfinals against the mighty Aussie team. He was once again the Man of the match.

The Aussies were a strong team nearly a decade. India had finally won against them.

It is significant after the epic defeat of India in the 2003 worldcup against Australia.We were all sure that India would win the tournament.

At last, our anxiety ended in happy tears when India won the 2011 World Cup. After the final match We forgot the restrictions we had in the hostel and celebrated the victory by shouting and dancing in joy. We burst crackers that we had bought with the help of the day scholars. We even heard noise from the usually quiet girls hostel. The warden had a tough time in bringing us back to normal.

I was so happy when Yuvi was announced as the Man of the Series. If asked who won the world cup for India 2011 the only right answer was Yuvraj Singh the fighter.

Because of the World cup fever in the hostel, we started playing cricket inside the rooms and I was the one who started it. I did it deliberately to have some quality time. And I knew that there would be one among us who would snitch later. As I predicted, I got caught for this and had to give many excuses. I waited patiently with a lot of efforts until I caught the spy. I formed a gang and gave a nice reply to him and made him run away from our room. After switching off the light,we gave our treatment and the spy got back his karma in his own way.

One night, we came down from the third floor room to stand in a line for study, then I saw a gang of boys standing and watching the backyard. I enquired them about the happening, one among them said, "There are a man and woman inside the lorry having their great time together" with a giggle. Just to show myself as a man of culture I told them that it was bad to peep, but I climbed the stairs quickly and threw the boys out of the way piercing through the crowd to see what was happening. Unfortunately, just as I came closer, the lights were put off. With a disappointed heart, I went to study. From then on every day I would go there and watch the lorry but I found nothing.

As I continued this, everyone in the room would stare at me I returned their look and said, "What do you want? Go and study." I knew that these adult things are the interesting talks of the age, especially in every boys' hostel. Those days as we didn't have television or smart phones, a lot of us entertained ourselves with Ouija boards to talk to the ghosts. The entire hostel would then start narrating ghost stories which freaked us like anything.

Still, I remember a story shared by one of my hostel friends, who grew up in the hostel since childhood, told us his late-night experience with Ouija board, He said he got up to go to the restroom that night when he saw someone there. He felt a knock on the door and as he opened he found no one. He shrugged it off thinking it might be his fear. He traced a shadow in the wall in front of him while he was relieving himself. There was no one again. He dreaded and rushed out of the washroom and took quick steps to return to the room. As he looked back, he traced a long hair image moving along as fast as he moved. Eventually, on reaching his room, he locked his door with shivered breaths and gasps. This story freaked out every one of us and then onwards we never went out of our room during midnight. We had all sorts of fun which every hosteler would have had.

After a few days, we received a blow of bad news that Suresh Babu sir was going to leave the school. I ran to his room to confirm on the news. He said he had a misunderstanding with one of the directors of the school and that made him resign his job. This was disheartening to me because he was the only motivator who helped me pick up a new ambition. I felt very bad about him leaving me alone in this school.A few weeks later the holidays were announced due to the 12th standard board exams for our seniors. We packed and returned home after a long time. I focused more on studies on these holidays. On my return, I sat with Elancheziyan and Sengutuvan in the EB2 class, the second topper class.

CHAPTER FIFTEEN

EXPOSURE

Kendriya Vidhayala,
Thanjavur.
2009

As my school was mainly for Central government employees, there were a good number of students from other states. They dominated in academics, sports and extra-curricular because they were all previously from Kendriya Vidhayalas all over India and they had a lot of experiences in adapting quickly to new environments. Most of them being Air Force brats was an added advantage for them.

They had experiences of getting transferred regularly and attending schools in different places. Apart from that, students were well versed in English as well as many other languages.

Some were intelligent as well as multi-talented compared to many of us who were book worms from kindergarten. There was a clear distinction between our maturity levels.

That year, the inter-school science exhibition was to be held at Kendriya Vidhyalaya in Tambaram, Chennai. Our

Principal was very particular that our school should participate in it. My class teacher approached my father who is a professor of chemistry, since they wanted a working model.My father got help from his friend Mr.Prabakaran who was a maths teacher.

He came up with the idea of measuring the height of an object using laser light and protractor with the help of a Trigonometry formula. I was forced to participate that time and besides no other student came up with their ideas.

I was ready with that model and Mrs. Rajappan, the wife of our Principal who was a primary grade teacher took me to Chennai by train along with a few other students and a teacher from Kendriya Vidhyalaya Trichy.

All the students from Trichy had quickly mingled and I struggled to do so with my poor English skills. I didn't want to expose my poor grammar skills and kept quiet throughout the journey.

We reached out sister institution in Tambaram where the competition was going to be held. It seemed bigger than my school and housed a lot of students from various districts as well as states, who hardly spoke English. I felt like an alien there because my teacher who was also from Kerala didn't know Tamil but somehow understood things.

In the science exhibition, I tried my best by explaining whatever was taught to me, but trigonometry was not a part of the 8th standard curriculum in CBSE. I failed to mug up all those formulas. I explained my complex project to the strangers to the best of my ability. I didn't have any help as my teacher had left me alone to loiter around.

In the exhibition, the judges asked about formulae and I admitted that I didn't know. I was not aware of who the judge was. When finally the judges came, I was so tired and did not have the energy to explain my project properly to them.

I simply just explained about my model and so I was not selected for the next round that was going to take place in IIT Chennai at the end of the day. I was not usually sharp, but when I made mistakes and I made sure to learn from them.

After the exhibition, the Trichy students went out without informing me and since my teacher was sleeping, I didn't want to disturb her. Without having much to do, I went to see the ground as usual. I saw a lot of happy faces roaming in groups and some even in pairs. I was the only person who stood alone in the whole ground. I had never felt such awkwardness and loneliness until then in my life.

That was when I also understood the importance of friends and language to connect with people. When I went to a classroom there was a couple who were kissing each other. I moved along immediately from there only to meet some of the most beautiful girls from Tamil Nadu and other states like Karnataka, Andhra and Kerala. I saw that all those girls had a fun time with the boys from their school. I had no one to speak to, and that day I wished I had a girl to speak to and laugh with.

Finally, I composed myself that there would be a girl in my life. I just didn't know where she was at the moment and hoped to meet her soon.

Like every guy, I was rocked by swelling emotions jealously as well as loneliness that day.

We returned to our school and as usual, I had a very bad time in passing Hindi. My Hindi teacher Mrs.Rama Verma always asked me and my Tamil friends to recite a Hindi poem. Despite mugging those lines, I'd blabber something in Hindi as soon as I was questioned.

She would make me stand outside the class and give daily homework to write that poem as punishment. For some days, my friends and I did and it didn't take long for us to lose interest as we started going out of class to play catch with a tennis ball and football with a water bottle.

One fine day, she caught us playing in the ground, and lodged a complaint to the Principal. He beat us black and blue with his favourite weapon of choice – a stick. Even after we had gotten all those beatings for our poor Hindi performance, we somehow passed 8th grade exams and moved to the 9th grade.

Then suddenly our old Principal was replaced by a Biology teacher , Mrs Mini Manoharan from Kerala. She was one of the reasons why I started loving biology. She was a good teacher. After her arrival, we received an announcement about the Inter-district KV cricket tournament at Karaikudi. I had waited for this news for a long time.

In one of our Biology classes, she asked if any of us had any doubts in the topic she had explained. I raised my hand and the whole class turned back to look at me. They were surprised that I had actually listened to the class to ask a question. I asked her, "Can we start a cricket team in the school?"

She smiled and asked me to meet her in the Principals office. She said there was no kit available or any of the things for Cricket, and asked us how would we play.

We said that we would somehow arrange for everything by ourselves and pleaded with her to just allow us to participate in the tournament. Being the good person that she was, she got funds from the government and allowed us to participate in that tournament with a proper school cricket kit.

My long cherished dream was finally happening in real life because I had switched two different schools for simply touching the new cricket ball that I was holding in my hand to bowl.

We went to Karaikudi, and it was the T20 tournament. Out first match was against Ooty. All 11 players in our opposing team looked like professional players, but we weren't rattled either, as our bowling department always gave their best.

Our only worry was that our batsmen weren't in their best shape. I was the opening bowler for the team along with Raja, as we both were in good form. Arun became the opening wicketkeeper and the team was is in full josh. We were all wearing our white jerseys with nicknames and I was wearing the name DADA with jersey number 5 that I had picked out.

We took them head-on in the first half, but just as predicted we lost the match because of our batting. In the next match against the team from Rameshwaram, even after taking 3 wickets for 12 runs in 4 overs in my bowling, we lost. We weren't able to control our top-order collapse.

Further, we played against Karaikudi, I was proud of taking 2 wickets for 20 runs in 4 overs. That day was no good either and we lost the match. Inspite of the poor performance from our team mates , Raja and I kept up with our strengths and were performing well.

The umpires were so impressed with our disciplined bowling and they enquired about us. We informed them that we were already playing in the Thanjavur district nets.

Finally, the last match was against Pondicherry that day. I had a good time with batting in the sixth down position and for the first time our team had a good score of 103 on the board, I scored 32 runs (not out) and Arun had a 33 run rate (not out) . It was a tough match and as Raja and I were the star bowling figures, I bowled 3 overs for 5 runs with 2 wickets while Raja bowled 3 overs 16 runs 3 wickets.

Pondicherry needed 16 runs in last 2 overs, and the match was almost in our control. And as Raja started the 19th over, I was waiting for the last over. Immediately, the whole moment of winning the match was out of our reach, as Raja lost his rhythm.

He bowled too many extras, and before we knew, it was a complete disaster and Pondicherry had won that game in the 19th over. The team was dejected at the loss and that incident made me realise that I should never wait to bowl the last over. If I had bowled the 19th over, it would have added a lot of pressure to the final over for the batsmen and things would have changed otherwise. But there was no one to coach our team. This tournamenthad taught me a lot of lessons.

As we left Karaikudi with a lot of emotions, we felt guilty informing our principal that we lost all the matches. But she took it easy and told us that this had been the first tournament and that we did not have to worry and have to prepare well for the tournament in the next years.

I returned to my district nets to face the same disappointment. Mr.X an important person in Thanjavur district cricket association , who had got his post by political influence usually came to the nets and batted an hour, while all the under 19 boys would bowl.

He did not know anything about batting but would pretend as if he were a great cricketer. During this daily drama, the Under-16 boys, had one task at hand - to retrieve the ball in nets and throw it to the bowler. This was pretty much the reason why Thanjavur district nets never produced any good player for the state team.

This X used the boys who played there as his slaves. His wife often called us to get parceled food from hotels as if we were her servants. Once I had informed this to my father and he immediately ordered me not to go that place anymore as there was no need to play a game in that manner. It was then that I stopped playing in the district nets.

Even now I see some of the boys around the nets picking up the balls, hoping that one day the fraudulent X would give them a chance to become a big player in the state team. But the boys were never going to understand that he would treat them like dogs.

CHAPTER SIXTEEN

MIRAGE

Kendriya vidhyalaya,
Thanjavur.
2009

After a few days, our school had a plan to participate in the Handball tournament that took place in Pondicherry. As the rules of the game were simple enough, we started practising hard. Unlike cricket, there wasn't a lot of competition for Handball and so we hoped to win the matches in Pondicherry which would lead us to the Regionals. Before the match, a big surprise awaited and this brought back the glimpse of my grandmother's superstitious words, "Catching the flying seed pods of silk cotton would bring exciting news."

Just as she predicted, the day I caught that seed truly turned out to be one of the best day. A junior came running to me and informed that I had been selected for Regionals in KV cricket tournament at Karaikudi. Yes, Raja and I had been selected for the regionals to represent Trichy region.

I wanted to share this happy news with my family and on hearing this my father was so happy. Like all mothers, my mom was not happy at the thought of me choosing sport over academics. I then informed the news to my maternal grandparents who were my favourite people in the immediate family. They keenly supported my interest in sports and even taught me about sportsmanship. After having been a government school PE teacher in Ammapet village in Thanjavur for so long, my grandmother told me her experiences and struggles she had faced which had taught her many lessons in life.

When grandpa had left the family to work out of town, she had struggled in nurturing the family by her hardwork . Despite all the struggles she was determined to provide education to her two sons and a daughter.She made them a doctor , an engineer and her daughter as a Physics graduate. She had also saved up money and had bought a house in Thanjavur so our grandparents could live near us in their old age. My childhood was colourful with the things I did with my grandparents when they visited us every Sunday. Apart from them, my paternal grandfather was a director of physical education in a government school. So it suffices to say that I had sports in my genes.

After receiving a whole lot of blessings, Raja and I left for Karaikudi again with our English teacher Mrs.Gita Ramesh. She had accompanied us since our PE teacher couldn't come. She ensured our parents that we would be safe.

There were two days of rigorous practice at Alagappa University in Karaikudi. The net practice was good with the head coach Mr. Swaminathan. He then called both of us separately and enquired where we hailed from and other details about our school and family.

Once the practice session was over, as Raja and I were walking towards the room, he gave a shocking news. He told me that the coach had taken us for walks separately to learn about our castes. I immediately asked him how he had figured that out.

"He touched my holy thread to check whether I was a higher caste or not. He must've done the same to you. Didn't he?" asked Raja. Only then I realized the reason behind the coach putting his hands around my shoulders and that day only I knew Raja was a Forward caste. It felt sick to even recall that memory.

The first match was a 50 over match against Chennai and I had carried my Yuvraj Singh card along with me in my pocket. I took that particular card from my cricket card set and had it with me as it was because of him, I was standing confidently on the ground. I wanted him to be with me while I played. Unfortunately, I was not part of the playing XI but Raja was in and I was happy that at least Raja performed well in our team. It came as a surprise to me because almost none of the other bowlers in the team had bowling stats like me and still they got to play while I was warming the bench. And I was also able to discover that since Karaikudi had conducted the tournament, it was obvious that most of the players belonged to their school team. I simply hoped for a chance in the future matches as it was evident that none of them had performed well.

The next day, to my shock and out of interest my father had come to Karaikudi to watch me play and yet again, the same team continued to play. I felt disappointed to have let my father down. He nevertheless encouraged me and told me that I would definitely get a chance the next day since it was the last day of the regionals and that all the players would be given a chance. My father couldn't stay back as he had only taken one day off from his work. I felt heartbroken having known that my father wanted to see me playing and that it was hard for him to watch me sit on the benches when the less talented and poor performing players played.

The following day that was the last match and I was in playing 11s, our team won the toss against Kozhikode team and decided to bat first. The first wicket fell in the very first over. It was expected that one of the three top-order batsmen would move to the crease but all I heard was, "Shreedher Priyan pad up next". Suddenly at that movement, the entire world seemed blank. Despite having three top-order batsmen who had padded up and sitting beside me, I went to the crease, took the guard only to hear one of the fielders' comment,

"He is fit for nothing".

The first ball I faced was a good full-length outswing delivery, that I couldn't touch. It was very hard to face the ball with the ragging comments and I had never practised for batting under such conditions. The fear of doing an unplanned and unprepared task just freaked me out I was not ready for it and I wanted to leave the field as soon as possible. After having struggled for two overs, I voluntarily gave my wicket for run out. As I returned to the pavilion, I saw a smile crossing my coach's lips. I was waiting for the second half to prove myself and kept my anger inside me to convert that in my strongest suit of bowling.

Even though, I was depressed but fully ready to bowl the next innings I wanted to prove them wrong. When the bowling session started, I waited for my chance, over after over. Having lost my patience, I walked up to the captain and asked him for a chance he gave a over and I bowled a maiden over but suddenly he stopped my spell without any reason. I believed that I was refused the chance because of my performance in the first innings batting.

I sat down in a stone bench alone and thought about what had happened, why and how it all happened to me.

I heard a voice next to me say, “Don’t feel upset Shreedher, it may look like you didn’t perform well but that wasn’t entirely true. You were made to perform bad.” I turned around and found the umpire of the match next to me.

I was puzzled by what he had said. He then continued once again. He told me, “I know about your skills. If you perform well they will be forced to select you to the next level. But they already have a plan of selecting particular people for the nationals. If I were your coach I will have made you play right from the first match. But your coach has taken note of your caste and has realized that you were not a forward caste. In Tamil Nadu, cricket can be categorized as a forward caste sport. Because of your fair looks and your name they might have thought you were a forward caste, but as and when they find out you aren’t, you will continue to be looked over unless you exhibit extraordinary talent. I cannot blame it all on them, since you wasted the one chance you got.”

I retorted back with malice and anger in my voice. " Who? Me? They gave me only a single over to bowl. How am I supposed to prove my skill then?

He replied, "They gave you a bat!"

“I never asked for it and I am not a batsman”.

"Why should they give you a chance only in bowling? You had 49 overs to bat. one should start hitting singles to get to 10s, one should collect ten 10s to get a century. Chances will not reach you as you wish, it will come in any form and you should have the attitude of utilizing it. You should catch any rope that is available to reach the mountain’s peak. You may be a good bowler but you should prove to be an all-rounder. I saw all your shots when you hit against Pondicherry and scored 32 runs. If you had given that performance today, you would be on your way up. The truth is you don't have the patience to wait for the wrong ball from the bowler and make use of those to score good runs. Your lack of patience and inability to adapt to the situation has made you sit here.

"Besides all this, I suggest that you quit cricket. Take up academics, read well, get a good job so you could be happy and make your parents proud. I say this because this game is not for other castes and I am the best example for it. If someone had explained about these caste politics when I was young, my life would have been completely different. I have lost my life because of cricket. I hope you can understand things at this age and decide correctly. You should remember one thing in your life, irrespective of your skills, you should not speak, your scorecard should speak for and about you."He got up and left.

Among the many things he said, there was one that caught my attention. *Opportunity never comes according to one's wish.* A person ought to catch any rope that is available instead of waiting for the correct rope to climb.

I then asked about this forward caste politics to Raja and he explained about it in detail. And I then understood everything to a point - my friend Karthik Narayan was a forward caste and his father was also a forward caste. Hence he became a cricket player. The coach Mr.Venkat was a forward caste and Mr.Swami Nathan was also a forward caste. All these politics had taken a long time for me to understand and I had to learn it the hard way. One question prevailed and bothered me. "*What next*?"

On returning to Thanjavur, I went to school and found myself lost somewhere in deep thoughts about the caste politics that I had been a victim of. My parents had noticed it, and they decided to change my school. It had been especially my mom's idea and I was not in a position to say yes or no. I knew one thing for sure though. No matter how many tournaments I would attend, there were chances that my bad experience would definitely repeat itself. I also thought about the other things that the good umpire had said.

I understood the reality and accepted the fact that I could never become a cricket player like my hero Yuvraj Singh. I confronted my father and said, "Don't cheat me anymore dad. Caste system and politics surrounding it exist in our country. You may not consider caste, but people are judging me based on the caste I belong to. So I must know who I am."

I decided to change my school again.

CHAPTER SEVENTEEN

REALITY

Maxwell School,
Thanjavur
2010

The first school that I had come out of, now I was returning there again. I had decided to go back to immerse myself in academics. The Principal Mr.Varadharajan had taken a look at me for a second and had accepted my admission magnanimously as I was an old student. It was common knowledge that schools never took admissions during 10th standard.

It had to be either during the 9th standard or the 11th standard. I knew this and thanked the Principal for his timely help. My mom then motivated me by saying, "You have the skill, diligence , good temperament, great character and flexibility. You can achieve well in academics".

On the first day after returning, I felt shy when I entered the school. I had left this school for my love for the playground and if my old friends found me back, they would troll me mercilessly for joining the school again. Apart from that I also had a few problems here.

When I was in my second standard, I got tensed and broke the head of my classmate by smashing his head over the desk during a fight. I am always calm and never lose my temper. But when I did loose control, I would beat my opponent mercilessly until someone pulled me away.

Eventually, the school management also wanted me to quit when the boy's parents came and made it an even bigger issue.

Stepping inside that old school, pretending to be a new student still brought back all those memories. I walked up to an empty table and sat alone quietly. I was glad that I was not noticed by my old friends who were there in the classroom. The only ones were the ones who had been admitted after I had left school.

Suddenly, a thunderous voice behind me shouted, " *Hey* Shreedher, *what are you doing here?*"

Holy shit! Someone had recognised me. Three of my best friends Vaitheeswaran, Anand karthikeyan and Dharmarajan from my fourth standard had caught me and immediately started their trolling. I pretended as if I didn't know them until they finally started beating me for my acting performance. But I had got my company again.

It was very hard to sit continuously here at this school. Because in KV we used to have atleast one PET period a day. Fate again pushed me into a cage. The only solace was that my grandparents' house was near to this school.

I always went home for lunch. They never failed to fill me up with food and snacks. And it was my duty to finish all of them compulsorily and that made me look like a fat pig. Without any physical activity and with the continuous hogging, my weight started to increase.

My grandpa was an amazing person. He would buy whatever I asked him but it was not limited only to me. He always helped everyone. Once when someone had asked him money for a hospital emergency, he gave his golden ring to them and never expected anything back from them. He was one of the innocent humans that I ever had met in my life. Every day my grandma narrated grandpa's stories of innocence and how some people took advantage of that to cheat him.

After school, I went back to my home in the evening, with my cycle. I pedalled from home to school and back with a lot of thoughts as it was around 8 kilometres away from each other. During this routine, I crossed the Kittu ground and would watch the cricket nets. I would wait as a spectator for a second to take look at the batsmen in the nets to identify their weakness and what would be an apt ball to bowl to get his wicket.I wished to play happily with them but somehow I will control myself and sadly start pedaling my bicycle to my house.

I tried hard to concentrate on my studies but it proved to be rather difficult as I constantly felt guilty for not having hit those 35 runs in Karaikudi. If I had done that, there would have been a chance for me in the next year's selections. And if I were selected, I would have used my scoreboard to beat those politics, because no one in that regional tournament had ever hit more than 40 runs.

I kept feeling like I had lost the one chance for a shot at what I loved and felt the opinions of the good umpire told about my skills was right. These thoughts were nagging at the back of my head and it prevented me from studying.

One day on my way back home, I saw a lot of crowd in nets. I went closer and heard that the coming Sunday was the under-16 selection. I came home not wanting to talk about it to my parents. My mom knew about it even before me and on seeing me confused, she asked, "What is bothering you?"

I said, "I'm not able to concentrate on my studies as I'm preoccupied." As a mother, she knew exactly what I needed, "There is an Under 16 selection in Kittu ground coming Sunday and I saw it in the newspaper. Go and participate.

When you come back you should have buried all the guilt of having lost an opportunity. You have got a new one. You have to promise me that if your attempt fails, you'll leave all this making-cricket-your-career nonsense behind and concentrate on your academics. Your aim should be to get yourself admitted in a good college and there you can play enough cricket."

It was my last chance to try.

Arun and I got selected by the Tamil Nadu Cricket Association for the District level Tournament in Theni. It was a one day match from 7 a.m. to 5 p.m. I was often disturbed by a thought that I would not be one among the players in the field.

Despite that I calculated the probability of playing as there were only three decent fast bowlers. I underwent a strenuous practice to pace myself in the field for an entire day which also helped me to reduce my weight up to 10 kgs and raise my stamina needed for this tournament.

I took up a lot of fitness drills to withstand but two days before the tournament, the saddest part was, we players who came to the net practice regularly and bowled thousands of deliveries to the in charge of the team were made as substitutes.

To our surprise a couple of new players from Pattukotai were introduced in our places. Just by looking at them, it was evident that they were older than us and had changed their ages. At that instant, my conscience questioned, "Are we fools here to play everyday? "

But then we went to the tournament where I had a company of Swathish, who was an opening bowler like me. He came from a similar family background like me. We did not get a chance to bowl as usual, during the first two days. It was like déjà vu. Every one of those so-called seniors played and lost the two matches. I counted on my chance in the third match against Theni.

One of the opening batsmen was blasting every bowler's delivery and I stood there calculating his foot work. I observed that he took a big front foot before the release of the ball. On the contrary, if it were a short ball, he adjusted and took a back foot to smash the ball.

So, I realised that we had to bowl slower balls to deceive him. I was watching out for my turn and finally got the chance to bowl 27th over. Around that time the ball had already been worn out and everyone was tired including the batsmen who had scored 85 runs.

I bowled the first ball with full pace in good length outside of off stump, and the next ball in full pace and full length outside of off stump. He missed both the balls as it was a fast-paced delivery. I predicted that he would come out of the crease to loft it over to the extra-cover region. I signaled the long-on to come in line with my wrist and I bowled a full length slower delivery to the stumps.

Just as I had predicted, he was deceived by the ball and gave a straight catch to me. And that was my first wicket!

No one in the ground knew that I waited for 27 overs to bowl to break their partnership. I sent a well-settled batsman to the pavilion.

Finally, it was at that moment in which I got satisfied with myself. I took the chance to once again show my swing bowling. After I finished rubbing that tattered ball, it shined for me to get some reverse swing. A fine swinging yorker got me another wicket in that match. Thus, I bowled 7 overs, conceded 18 runs and took 2 wickets. Even though we lost the match, personally I was satisfied with my performance.

I related the day to the words of my previous coach, 'One should always go in the flow of luck and accept that everything cannot be under our control at all times. Based on luck, every bowler will have three different days of experience in matches.

A good player will be able to figure out the worst, ordinary and the best days at the very beginning. On a worst day, if you cannot pitch the ball in the right areas, control your swing or your extras, accept that it is not your day and try sticking back to your basics.

"A cross seam delivery will be the right choice which mostly gives singles and not look bad in your score card."

'The second type of experience is the ordinary day which will also be the case in most of your matches. On feeling this, bowl your normal deliveries without an extra pace or swing to the best of your ability giving it all based on the practices.

The last type of experience is nature's gift. When you are in the right form with the perfect rhythm along with luck's favour, utilize it to the fullest. Try as much as possible to take an extra pace and an extra swing to capture wickets to become the star performer of the day.'

I cheered myself up but Swathish was so upset as he never got a chance to bowl. I calmed him saying that it was only his first experience.

Later that day, I was eager to know my future in cricket and so I asked Mr.X who accompanied us, "How I could get myself into the Tamil Nadu Ranji team". He simply told me,

"Give me 2 lakhs, I will take care of the rest." He did not stop there. With a sarcastic tone, he asked again, "Can you afford it?" with a smirk in his face.

I just smiled and thought to myself these greedy beggars had this sarcasm only because I belonged to the middle class. I told myself that I would make them look up to me one day when I become wealthy.

Yuvaraj too was not interested in cricket in his earlydays.But out of his father's compulsion he came to this field. His entry in the Cricket made him popular and fetched pride to the nation. Likewise some other field is waiting for me to achieve.

Though I was satisfied with myself I understood the reality. In those days, I had to be as a son of a millionaire or a minister or a forward caste to enter into Tamil Nadu cricket. You might assume this as the rant of someone who couldn't make it big, yet it is the truth.

So just as I had promised my mother, I took up academics seriously soon after the match to prove myself and managed to get 448/500 marks in my 10th grade board exams which looked much lower compared to my abilities. I scored the least of 78 marks in English. Right from the start, my English teachers would scold me for my grammar mistakes and I still struggle to talk or write in proper grammar. But to all my teachers' surprise and to my surprise, here I am doing the unexpected feat of managing to release an English novel with a help of a team.

After the board exams, I felt that I should have some changes in my environment. So I purposefully asked my parents to admit me into one of the Namakkal residential schools.

My parents were tired of changing schools, and they said that they wouldn't be able to speak with Maxwell school's

Principal. I took my time and went to talk to the Principal.

I explained how I felt about my situation. He understood and gave me the Transfer certificate. I thanked him wholeheartedly and the started the Namakkal mission from where this novel started.

I had to do something different to forget my past. Even if I failed, I would have something new to feel about instead of the old ones that kept haunting me.

BACHELOR OF CRICKET

CHAPTER EIGHTEEN

EXHAUSTED

Greenpark,
Namakkal.
2012

I returned to EB2 a second topper class after my summer holidays got over. A strange fear lurked inside me as I saw all my new studious classmates. I sat in the last bench as usual. Since Suresh Babu sir had left our school, there was no one to personally motivate me.

The only other good thing apart from him was one of the school's directors. Mr. Mohan was my Maths teacher for EB1 class. He was a wonderful teacher but a strict disciplinarian and was always on time and expected the same from us.

Just as we thought the days were going fine, another disaster set foot. There was an outbreak of chicken pox in our hostel. Since I had gotten typhoid previously, I was susceptible to this disease. Nonetheless I requested the warden to let me go home in order to distance myself from those infected. He replied, "If you leave then everyone will want to go. So I suggest you stay here". As expected I got chicken pox.

Finally I was allowed to go home for about two weeks by that stupid school. It had been a hell of a time at home both physically and mentally. I was tired all the time and slept sixteen hours a day for most days, which left me clueless about what had happened in those fifteen days.

Once I was feeling better, I came back to school. I had to cover a lot of chapters from the classes I had missed . And I came to know there were unit tests in a few days. The break had completely spoiled my academics and I struggled to even pass. My confidence was let down and I was losing every reason to study hard. Inspite of that I continued to work and study as hard as I could to get myself back in track with my academic marathon in which I had been pulled far back by chicken pox.

I worked like a robot. Woke up, read - ate – slept, got poor marks andthe vicious cycle continued. The study whistle, which was the wake up call in the morning, irritated me so much that I ended up hating those sounds throughout my life. Some days all of us continued sleeping even after hearing the whistle continuously. I decided that not to hear the sound of a whistle in my life after finishing school.

Just as if this weren't all enough to spoil my mood , we were asked to shift to a new hostel still under construction. There weren't enough cots available and some of us were asked to adjust and sleep on the floor for two weeks till the first floor got ready.

Every guy ran to the new hostel as if their very life depended on it to secure a cot for himself. I couldn't even try because I was weak and tired. As I shifted in my own pace, the one who got there fast got lucky. By the time I reached there all the cots were already taken.

The rooms were small like the bathrooms of my previous hostel with four double decker cots. It was very difficult just to accommodate eight members into it along with all their belongings and I happened to be the unfortunate ninth member.

I thought it couldn't get any worse; only to be proven wrong again. I was put in a room full of toppers who neglected me and disrespected my very existence. I cleaned the dirty floor to put my bed while giving some space for the others to walk around. The only information that kept me going was that I had to adjust to this for another ten days and after which I will be able to move into a new room.

Within two days, I felt my room mates neglecting me. They felt irritated, purposefully misbehaved with me by walking over my bed with their shoes.

I screamed, "Don't walk on my bed with your shoes."

"What are we to do if you put your bed in the pathway?" replied a boy from the gang.

"Remove your shoes while you enter the room" said I. He said he wouldn't and continued the same.

I controlled my urge to beat him. If I had given in to my urge, he wouldn't have any teeth to speak again. I was reaching the peak of my frustration. I couldn't study that entire week with all this nuisance and on the eighth day I had had enough.

The same guy stood over my trunk box to take something from the shelf. I asked him not to do that and before he could respond, my anger got burst. I punched his nose and blood splurted from it. I lost all my cool that I had maintained over many days. I picked him up by the collar of his shirt.

My calm was the one that came before a storm. A person with enough to accomplish and worry about in his own life would never bother others. When such people are troubled beyond their limits, they hit back and nobody can handle it.

That guy had crossed his limits. I kept thrashing him with the intention of putting him into a forever sleep. One of his friends tried to push me away from him. I hit with such force that he cartwheeled out of the room. Seeing my ferocity the others in my room were frozen and did not even attempt to stop me.

I looked at them. With a voice laced with rage,

I shouted , "Which one of you said you'll walk only on my bed? Who said that he can't find space on the floor? I dare you to come forward now. If anyone of you step on my bed I'll cut your feet. The beating I gave him is a warning for all of you. Are you all big heros just because you got some extra marks than me? So it's enough in life if you get marks alone you b***?"

My friends from EB3 took me to their room after coming to know my theatrics.

When the next shuffling happened, I ran like Usain Bolt and got myself a room with roommates I knew. Elancheziyan became my roommate once again. Happy with the set up I started to complete the lessons for which I had to take a sprint in this race in order to cover the portions.

The mental pressure that existed in us drastically increased. Unfortunately, some could not cope up with that and it landed them in problems often. The person who experienced this personally was the guy I had thrashed badly. He was in the topper class.

He had evident changes in his activities. When the others started noticing it, they started teasing by calling him as psycho. To be honest, I felt my physical beating was far better than all the teasing and the mental trauma the others were causing him.

He started avoiding people. As our new hostel did not have proper gates he went out to a construction site nearby and read on top of a sand hill. On seeing this, students would scream on the top of their lungs calling him psycho. I felt that the real psychotic people were those who continued to tease him after knowing he had some mental health issues . I had soon felt guilty for having fought with him without knowing his condition.

One day, the boys started throwing stones at him as he was reading. I rushed to save him from the pelting and to support him with my words. As soon as he saw me, he started running towards the exit gate and this gave the students one more reason to giggle and hoot.

Soon after this the warden was informed, and he rushed with the watchman and caught the boy from escaping. The boy cried as he was brought back to the hostel. I felt bad on seeing that. I then understood how the pressure to study well could worsen someone's mental state.

The boy's parents were called and were advised to take him to a psychiatrist for counselling. Surviving in the hostel like Namakal school, needed a great mental strength and to come out on top needed much more.

Sometimes as I sat alone the very first thought was about Yuvraj's health because I heard that he had gone in for his cancer treatment. I prayed everyday for his speedy recovery and wished to meet him in person just to tell him how much he had inspired me in my life.

Even as he was hospitalised he continued to inspire me by fighting back the cancer with his own Punjabi attitude. My final wish was that he should come back and play for India again.

In the middle of all this, I got homesick myself with the tough situations and competition. I badly wanted to talk to my mom and dad. But the rules didn't permit me.

We were allowed only one phone call per week. This paved the way for a new habit of mine. I started to write daily to let out my emotions. And this led me to write this novel later in my life.

When I came back after the vacation, I brought a Nokia basic model mobile from home to speak with my parents. Sengutuvan was a day scholar, he would take my phone to charge it and give it back to me as there were no charging points in our hostel. It became my own little secret!

CHAPTER NINETEEN

FIGURING OUT

Namakkal.
2011

After our seniors had finished their exams, our results came. A lot of students had scored above 195/200 which was enough to get a medical seat in government quota.

Each subject had an exam for a total of 200 marks. The medical cut off was calculated for 200 marks. Biology marks were converted to 100 whereas Physics and Chemistry marks were converted to 50 marks each and all the three were added up.

If one had a cut off of 198 or more, they would definitely get into a government college. The fees was a maximum of 20,000 rupees for an entire year.

If someone had a cut off of 195 or more then only they would get a government quota seat in a private medical college. The student had to spend 5-6 lakhs per year as fees.

If the cut off was less than 195, then such candidates had to buy their way into a private medical college under the management quota by paying a capitation fees (or a donation , if you wanted to be diplomatic) . That capitation fee itself came to 50 lakh rupees (or more if the candidate wanted to join close to the final date of admission) and an annual fees of 10 lakhs for the entire course duration of five years. There was no way my family was going to be able to afford such an insane amount of money.

There were pamphlets with the names and photos of those who had scored a medical cut off of 195 and above. There were banners with the photos and details of those who had achieved a cut off of 197 and above. Whenever I saw those banners, I would imagine my name and photo in them the next year.The school took the privilege of printing the rank holders achievements in pamphlets and banners.

As I shared this with a few boys, the rest of my classmates walked up to me and told me that I shouldn't think of studying with them. They reasoned that they belonged to a particular caste and they would place themselves easily with their quotas which in turn would end up in a tragedy for me. That is when I realized that all the castes had their separate gangs even inside my classroom. The forward caste students had a separate gang and had their discussions. It was then that I comprehended there were reservation percentages if one has to go to college. I aimed to score a 197.75 medical cut off so that I could choose a government college somewhere in Tamil Nadu. I wanted it to be flexible when it came to the choice of college, as I believed in one's ability more than the institution's ability. Therefore, I did not have a stubborn mentality to study only in Madras Medical College.

The academic year was yet to get over but classroom teaching was finished . We were left to self- study in our study hours. As I stepped on to the track of my final race, I thought it is now or never.

On this positive note, I started proceeding with my plan but fell short of time. I failed to finish the portions I planned each day. I concluded that the extra hours were the only solution. So I started waking up at 4 a.m every day to study for an extra 2 hours.

It did not last long. The sleep of my roommates was disturbed due to the lights switched on early in the morning. I buckled up to study near bathroom area lights. The constant noise of all those who were showering prevented me from studying.

After a week of that, I had had enough. I walked to Mohan sir and asked him, “Please permit me to go to school at 4 a.m.”

He rejected the request stating, “I cannot appoint a special study in-charge just for you.”

I said, "I don’t want any study in-charge, sir."

" Even if you don’t, I cannot allow you to study alone in school. Try reading in your hostel otherwise wait for two more months and by then we will be back to the waking up time to 5 a.m. And this is final!” said he.

I was clueless about how to proceed apart from continuing to study at school hours. The rat race amongst us started at 6 a.m. every day. We had only two breaks during the *seventeen* hours of study – one for breakfast at 7:30- 800 a.m. and another for lunch at 12:30 -200 p.m.After finishing our lunch we had some time to shut our eyes. 1 hour of sleep was needed for us to concentrate for the next *nine* hours from 2 PM to 11 p.m. If by chance we lost that 1-hour sleep, we would end up feeling drowsy and tired the rest of the day. I got into trouble often as I was a light sleeper. And as our room was just below the place where new construction was going. Hence the noise was inevitable. All my roommates had the gift of sleeping deep and nothing seemed to ever disturb them. Whereas I would wake up even to the slightest of sounds and would stay awake as I could never get back to sleep after waking up.

The construction workers started their work sharp at 1.30 PM after their lunch. As they drilled their machine, I tried inserting cotton plugs in my ears to block the noise. When that didn't work, I tried sleeping with a pillow over my head. I even requested the people concerned to postpone the work but nothing worked out in my favour. So I decided not to have lunch and left directly to my room. I start sleeping at noon and I would be awoken by the sounds at 1.30 PM . I couldn't go to the mess as it would be crowded with 11th standard students.

As a result of all the starvation, I developed peptic ulcer which started causing severe hunger pains randomly during the day and night. The pain was too high to manage, especially at night. It was highly difficult to have snacks in boys hostel. Once snacks was spotted, the guys would devour it in a minute like a pack of ravenous wolves. One could never say no to those who ask for food and I did not want to hide those snacks. Eventually, my stomach got used to it and I started the countdown for the final exam. There were 200 days left before the final board exams.

I bunked a few study hours when the situation became very hard to handle. I would leave saying that my stomach was upset and as I was excused, I rushed to call my mother secretly with my mobile inside the hostel. I spoke in detail about the situation and explained saying, "I don't think I can make it here mom. Everything that happens seems to be against me and I do not know how to tackle it."

She came up with a bold idea and said, "Wake up at 4 AM, go to the study hall in your school without asking anyone. If and when a problem arises, we will see about it then. Sometimes we ought to take risks on our own to succeed. Even if you get caught, I will come there when your Director calls and argue that there is nothing wrong with what you are doing. So go ahead and take the risk."

That simple conversation with my mother motivated me. It gave me hope and the strength needed to rebuild myself. I slept that night planning for the right time to make a move the next morning.

You are much taller than you look
Toil on until you reach your goal
The pain that you have to face will be little death
Hesitate to hesitate
Return like a storm

Shake the heart until you reach the final round
It will lift you up and fan out in space
The magic key will take you somewhere
The magic key will lift you up
- Poet Vivek

CHAPTER TWENTY

FEARLESS

Namakkal.
2011

As I woke up at 4 AM the following day, I was set to execute my plan. My hostel gates were never locked as it was newly constructed, so crossing them was easy. The only problem was the school gate which was opened only during the school timings. It was 10 feet high compound wall. There was no way for me to get inside without a ladder.So I have to climb school gate and other side of the gate watchman was sleeping.

I had to be very cautious because there were two dangerous possibilities of me getting caught. If the watchman saw me with books in my hand, he might think I was escaping from the hostel and would raise the alarm by blowing his whistle. The second one is, I might have caught in many CCTV cameras installed there. In order to avoid all that, I had to cheat both the watch man and the CCTV.

I planned a plan and executed the same. I neared the gate and spotted that the watchman was sleeping. Without making any sound, I climbed on to the grill gate, stepped on to the compound wall, walked on the wall silently for around 8 feet. I threw my books on top of the sand mound kept for construction near to the wall, and jumped into sand mound from the compound. It was definitely not an easy task. It was then I thought about all the games that the players had to win the fun game "*Takeshi's Castle*' on Pogo channel. I smiled at myself for the tasks that I had to do to score good marks. Then I walked towards the front side of the school and slipped into my study hall in the ground floor and sat down. From that day I followed the same plan as my academics were at stake. Some days I got injured when I jumped into the sand mount but I never bothered it for the sake of improving my academics.

To be honest, it wasn't a peaceful experience. Being alone in a humongous building before the sun came up, made the brain see many things that weren't there.

After a few days, I heard footsteps as if someone was approaching the class. I thought it was the watchman and hid under the desk. The sound immediately stopped and I walked to the door to see who it was. To my surprise, nobody was there. I went to check on the watchman and he was sound asleep. The next day I heard the same sounds and I was petrified. I later composed myself saying it was all the mind's game of hallucinating the worst. In the end I got used to those sounds that I would not have been frightened even if a ghost had really visited me.

When I woke up early and step inside the washroom to freshen up, the area often resembled an insect habitat. There was one particular insect "Eri Poochi" that came from the graveyard behind the school ,1000s of those swarm over me when I enter washroom,one of which I was ignorant of, left a scar when it landed on the skin. A lot of students had been bitten and they underwent immense pain and had big scars. The most irritating fact was that the insect could fly and one had to take precautions to avoid the insect from landing on the skin. Every day as I went to the washroom, I was an one-man army against the hundreds of those devil insects that attacked me. I always carried a writing pad to use as a shield. Inspite of my best precautions, an insect entered my shirt collar and bit me on the shoulder. The scar is still visible till date . The pain had become unbearable which then pushed me to the practice of using the washroom after sunrise as the insects disappeared soon after sunrise.

One day while I jumped down from the compound as routine, a watchman caught me red-handed. I rushed to him to explain what I was doing and why. Fortunately, the good-hearted watchman understood my situation and told me the most incredible thing. "Do not jump compounds hereafter. Wake me up and I will open the gate for you. But do not talk about this to anyone". It was then that I understood there were some good people present around me. He also went one step ahead and brought tea for me while I studied.

One day he told me, “Once you become a doctor, please do give a free consultation to poor people at least one day in a week.” I was touched by his noble intent and promised to do so. From there on, I continued my sprint doubling upthe speed day after day. Many of my fellow students continued their marathon until midnight when I slept. They thought that I was falling behind. But they had grossly underestimated the fighter in me working in early morning.

August 31, 2011

We were not allowed to go home as the crucial exam time was nearing. Instead, our parents were allowed to come and meet us at school. On one such outing, the most expected movie of actor Ajith Kumar's "*Mankatha*" was released. I asked my parents to permit me to go with my friends. But then I felt immense guilt as I had dragged my parents all the way from Thanjavur to Namakkal since school allowed the students outside only when their parents showed up. Sengutuvan, had promised that he would buy tickets for the matinee show. I had lunch with my parents at a good hotel comfortably. We went to the theatre and Sengutuvan said that he couldn't get the 2 p.m. tickets but tickets were available just for the 6 p.m. show. The only problem was that I had to get back to my hostel by 7 p.m. and if I were to turn up late, Mohan sir would not let me inside the hostel. I planned to drop the plan of watching the movie, but my dad asked me to go to the movie and assured me that he would convince Mohan sir. I was grateful for that.

The teens in Tamil Nadu have been ardent followers of two actors named Vijay and Ajith for many years. Despite being a fan of Vijay I also admired Ajith. As all of us sat in the edge of the seat, the opening scene was dominated by with the virtuoso Yuvan Shankar Raja's music. The stylish entry of the hero Ajith made the whole crowd whoop and holler. I joined in by removing my t-shirt and waving it above my head and shouting at the top of my voice. The movie was a complete stress buster and the background score gave me goosebumps. The movie was no doubt a mass entertaining blockbuster. After the movie, my father took me to Mohan sir. He scolded me for being late. My dad argued with Mohan sir that he had travelled all the way from Thanjavur only to spend time, atleast half a day, with his son. The argument continued for a while. I pressed my father's hand and signaled him to stop arguing. After getting an apology letter, Mohan sir allowed me into the hostel by 10 p.m.. After that my parents took bus from

Namakkal to Thanjavur. My mom was so tired that time and I prayed god to make her happy with my results for all the efforts that she was taking to encourage me.

As I woke up at 4 a.m. the next morning, all I could hear was the music from the movie. It had entered my head and conquered my soul. I could not explain how it helped me but it boosted my mood whenever I listened to it. I became a huge fan of Yuvan Shankar Raja and many of us were addicted to listening to that particular Mankatha theme song.

My go-to song needed for motivation was '*Nimirnthu nil*'song by Gangai amaran.

Stand up and go bold
Start your era
Do what you think
Thought is your strength

Break down barriers
Leave the delays
Duties are new
Time will not change for you
You have to change according to time
As time goes problems dissolve and you will progress

Your life is in your hands, your speed is in your chest
Here is a test for your braveness
Rest and collide
At the end of the climb, your forces will win

Whenever I used to feel bad and wonder what life was going to be about, I used to recall the lyrics of 'Oru nalil' song written by N. Muthukumar.

Life in a day will not run anywhere
If the day comes again
Suffering will not continue
How many crores of tears poured on this earth
Yet earth make flowers to bloom here

When you walk at night,your shadow will also leave you
You are the only companion to yourself
Just see for the shore
We will wait on the ship
Even if the volcano erupts
Let's stand up and fight

Apart from these the inspiring words from the works of Dr.APJ Abdul Kalam such as "Those who say reasons never win " were etched in my mind. These lines motivated me during hard times.

As the exams neared no one had time to motivate others. To be honest, one couldn't afford the time to motivate someonein that tight schedule. We had to self-motivate and on that account, I wrote the lyrics of those songs in my books and read them whenever I needed them. I wrote my model exams in a fairly satisfying way and awaited the results of my hard work

CHAPTER TWENTY-ONE

MIND GAMES

The model exam results came. And I was disheartened to know that I had scored very poor marks. They were very less than what I had expected.

On reviewing my papers, I understood that I had done some silly mistakes such as not attending a 5-mark question in Physics inspite of knowing the answer to that question very well. I felt that the mistake happened due to the mental pressure.

My scores became a huge setback for me even though I had put my sincere effort. From there on, I felt down and lost the hope of securing a seat in a medical college. My vision became shades of black and white. Everything around seemed depressing.

At the same time, too many things added to my depression. The hostel maintenance was very poor and the school management did nothing to bring the situation under control. The washrooms in the school block became unbearable to use. I complained about it to the people in-charge many times. As per my plan, I could not even finish my morning ablutions at 4 a.m before studying. Apart from this, the old watchman had left his job without informing anyone, my phone was confiscated by the hostel warden and Sengutuvan also got into trouble because of me. I felt guilty for putting him in such a situation and as a compensation, I arranged for another mobile from a day scholar.

It was then when I noticed that people to whom I got close in that school were not permanent. The dog I used to play with and feed vanished suddenly. Suresh Babu sir and the watchman who had helped me had come into my life for only a short period, motivated me as much as they could and had disappeared. I realized that the only person I could rely on was myself. I decided that I need not depend on anyone. The truth is we cannot always depend on someone for constant support in our lives. We perceive that the one who shows steady progress as the strong-hearted person. But the truth is that the one who have faced a series of failures yet continues to work hard without expectations is the really strong-hearted person. I wanted to be such a strong hearted person.

"There will be no god if everything you think will definitely happen
You can't be in peace if you keep on thinking what happened
Understanding the change will clear the dizziness "
- Poet Kannadasan

After the results, all my mind could think about was Maths, Physics, Chemistry and Biology. Though I did not like Maths, I tried to give it my best shot,if I fail to get a 197.75 medical cut-off my only choice would be getting a seat im a good Engineering college. For which I had to score atleast a decent Engineering cut-off because my family could not afford to pay for self-finance or management quota for

MBBS. Several lakhs might be easy for the rich students in my school. Such students could pass in their exams with minimum marks and their parents would arrange for a seat in a private medical college by paying hefty donations. Those privileged few could become doctors even if they scored around 700 to 800 marks out of 1200 irrespective of the medical cut- off mark.

Another problem was this medical cut off in board exams would be your cut off forever. Another way was to write a national level entrance exam to get into a medical college in the All India quota. That was way tougher when compared to this board exam.

When these thoughts came, I suffered from emotional outbursts. I rushed to the bathroom to sit with the tap running and let out my stress by crying. One such day, some sadist guy dared to pour hot water on me when I was inside the bathroom. I came out and beat him with whatever I could lay my hands on. He immediately stopped me to explain that he had mistakenly poured it thinking that his friend was inside. I had to deal with such psychos in the hostel and sometimes one had to experience the horror of seeing two boys together in a bathroom.

My routine was simple. I went to school, got back to the hostel and left the room only for eating and using the restroom and spent the rest of the time studying. So far, I never saw anything that were far from me. Like me many of the students got vision impairment. All I had to see were three buildings (Hostel,Mess and School) and the books.

On one of these days I did not understand a problem in Physics. The Physics teacher for my class was absent that day. Only the teacher named PP who handled Physics for the toppers EB class was there.

I had never spoken to him till then. With a lot of hesitation I approached him. He taught me well and cleared my doubts. The following conversation happened after that :

"You didn't even know this. What did you read in school till now ? What is your ambition? "

" Sir I want to be a doctor"

"You need a high cut off to join MBBS. These sort of problems should be at the tip of your fingers. You are wishing beyond your level. Which class are you currently in?"

"EB1 sir"

"EB1 huh? I've never seen you in that class"

"I came to EB1 from EB3 after shuffling sir"

"Ok ok... Go read properly. You'll manage to get into some decent engineering college."

When that teacher said the last line whatever respect I had for him and the self esteem I had vanished into thin air.

I went to my room and thought deeply. I wasn't able to understand why he chose to disrespect me even without knowing anything about me. I could not make heads or tails about the way things were happening in my life. When I was in EB3 life sent a Zoology teacher across my path and motivated me. Now when I was in EB1 it sent this horrible Physics teacher to demotivate me.

I could have given back to that teacher with a snide comment but I held myself back. I wanted to give my reply in action, rather than words.

Sometimes rage was the greatest motivator in life. If we let it go then it was hard to get it back. Many of those who achieved big in life were those who underwent hardships, and embarrassment in their lives.

Within a few days, I lost my Zoology book somewhere in the school and it was one of my worst times in those two years of boarding. I had written far too many important things in my books such as my mnemonics and stuff that I had created on my own. When I lost it, I felt everything was happening against me and to add to my woes, there were no new books available in the school store nor were my friends ready to share their books with me.

I also lost my bucket, watch and the uniform that showed that I was not in my six senses, I was more confused and lost myself in that race. I called my dad and asked him to send a zoology book through a courier service as soon as he could.

Meanwhile, I couldn't study zoology. One of my friends had found someone's book in a random classroom without a name and so gave it to me. When I hesitated, my friend simply rejected my concern by saying that it was some boy's fault for loosing it. Instead of just taking the book, I searched for its owner, handed it to him and preferred to fail in the zoology test.

It was just who I was and who I am. My heart can withstand failure but it cannot withstand thoughts of betrayal and deceit. I soon got my new book and once again started marking important questions and notes to remember things easily.

Often I came to a point of giving up my efforts and decided that I couldn't do it anymore. I would go to the study room but not study anything. All I wanted was for my mind to be peaceful. I found myself in hell and did not want to achieve anything great with my life. I just wanted to eat good food and have a good night's sleep with a decent salary nothing more.

The one who just struggled daily to eat bread is sleeping inside the soil
And the one who daily ate feast also sleeping inside the soil
This is life to live
Nothing we had brought in our hand at birth to carry while death
- Poet Vairamuthu

As these thoughts came, my past popped up in my mind and forced me not to quit. It reminded me that I had crossed the halfway point of the marathon and it was not the time to quit. I realized that I had to complete this race irrespective of the result. On seeing everyone going past me in the race, I rose once again after a long halt and started to crawl with my hands. I suppressed my emotions and forced myself to be responsible 24 x 7. I didn't not have any time to waste.

You flow like a river ..
Success will count all your sweats..
If you sow today, you will reap tomorrow.
Do not forget it ..
God knows all the truth and pain that you go through now
You just leave it to him
- Poet Pa Vijay.

Out of the lakhs of students who applied for medical college counselling each year, only 2200 candidates would be able to avail the seats in the Govenment medical colleges in various cities across the state. I had to pass with nearly perfect scores if I wanted to be one of them. It was what almost everyone aimed for and worked like robots for.

At times like these, everything blurred inside my head, including who I was or what I was doing. One could think only about how much to study in a particular period. We hardly took breaks nor spoke to each other even while eating food . We hardly took five minutes to have our food and rushed back to our study rooms. I had a good plan and tried to execute it successfully till the last minute before the exams.

The only hope that I had was 'If tragedy can happen without any reason or logic, then why not success happen?

Every human in the world had certain characteristics which made them unique. But when put in a competition, the manner in which one handled the loss makes most people end up loosing their human nature and the beast inside us gets dominant. This in turn makes us to cross the mental barriers we had previously built in our minds which limited our potential. Yes! That beast mode has always distinguished the winner from others. Consistent hard-work is all we need and I learnt this from cricket, that being good was never enough. One had to be more than just good and had to keep on adding perfection to one's skill. It was necessary to satisfy your reward centre in the brain. I had turned on the beast mode inside me to master the subjects of Physics, chemistry and Biology.

Consistent hard work was the need of the hour. I had learnt this from cricket.

When we bowl the ball does not have to travel fast and with force just because the bowler had run with speed and effort till the crease. How we time the jump and the release of the ball would determine how fast the ball will travel.

My run up might have been slow but I would bring the pace with the jump I was going to make.

The beast within you think to fall asleep
If it wakes up ,Volcanoes erupt

It will ask you to feed the dreams
Then it will swallow you and
give yourself in your hands

Without burning you won't get honey
The ball will not rise without kicking
Pain is what survives
This is the rule of nature until now

If you live in hell ,
you have the only option of becoming a beast
After repeated cuts ,rise your head again and again

There is no friend here
There is no enemy to oppose
You are always your friend
You are always your enemy

Often you have to die
To reborn again
- Poet Na.Muthu Kumar

CHAPTER TWENTY-TWO

THAT'S WRAP

I was finally at the end game. My exams started. I did my Tamil and English exams well. My bench mate asked me to help him during the Physics exam as he was weak in the subject. I readily agreed with a condition that he should help me in Maths exam.

During the Physics study time, we got a lot of guidance regarding questions to be written and the questions to be left out while writing the examination. I took enough time to revise all my earlier answer papers to avoid the careless mistakes I had committed earlier. Some of our boys were getting easily distracted since the exam hall had both boys and girls. After having lived 2 years of life surrounded with boys only , sitting with the girls had brought about a lot of excitement. It was the same case in the girls too. After every exam, we had a chance to have a little talk. But I purposefully avoided that because I realised the importance of the big opportunity that was in my hands and I did not want to lose it for a mere attraction.

I entered into the exam hall like a racehorse on the track. I saw the physics question paper but that was not the one that was expected. There were completely new one mark and three mark questions. On seeing the question paper, my bladder started troubling me. It was so bad that within the 3 hours of the examination I had to go to the washroom eight times and invigilator started suspecting me of cheating. At one point he even sent someone to monitor me in the washroom as my panic had become evident.

I still had to work something out. As I wasted time for shunting between exam hall and wash room, I decided to write down the five and ten mark questions which require short span of time , so that I could have enough time to think and write the one and three mark questions at the end.

Finally, I solved out most of them with my knowledge and I was a little satisfied. It was a tough paper and I did my best. The only thing that troubled me was that I didn't have enough time to re check what I had written.

When I came out of the hall, a number of girls were crying because of the tough question paper. I did not stand a minute there and rushed back to the hostel. I planned to sleep for 2 hours in order to begin study for the Chemistry exam which was a few days away. I realized the mistake that I had committed in the physics exam. I panicked when I remembered that I forgot to check the number of five mark questions that I had written. I ran and called my mother through phone. I started crying as soon as I heard her voice. She asked me to check with my question paper and I refused, stating that if in fact, I had not attended the question. I feared that I would feel terrible and would not do well in my other exams. She asked me to calm down and study well for the next exam. With a weak heart, I did.

The next day morning while I was brushing I remembered that I had attended all the five mark questions and it came as a huge relief to me.

My schedule for studying Chemistry went as planned. I did well in the exam. I was hoping to get a perfect score.

My bladder started misbehaving again in the Maths exam. On the belief that my bench mate would help me, I tried to calm down. But he did not respond to my call at the exam. It was a betrayal in purest form (as far as the exams were concerned). After calling him repeatedly, I got irritated and pulled one of his papers.

To my horror, the flying squad(teachers who went randomly to all exam halls and whose sole job was to catch cheats) caught me ,they know I never copied anything from that paper and so they left scolding me for ten minutes. They warned me that if caught again I'd be debarred from the exams for the next three years. Following that I never tried asking anything from anyone and finished the exam. It was later that I got to know that the person who scolded me was not a member of the flying squad but the IAS officer of Namakkal district. It was sheer luck that I was allowed to write the exam.

Finally, for my Biology exam, I had planned to study Botany for a day and the rest for Zoology which required more time. The thought that the next day was the final exam to all the students, flashed a moment in my mind for. It was a day that we had dreamt ,every day for the past two years. It gave me a jubilant mood because I felt like a prisoner during this entire period of two years stay in this school. I couldn't wait to get it over with.

I woke up at 4 AM revised some portions and had a small power nap at 6 AM. Before entering the exam hall, I saw a flying cotton seed, caught it and put it into my pocket. I took that as a good omen.

I was thorough with the chapters of Biology and so I did the exam to my satisfaction. I stepped out the classroom with a smile that stretched across my face. When it was finally over, the boys and girls exchanged their phone numbers, some even professed their feelings to their crushes. There were a lot of emotions involved, with some laughing and some crying. I ran to my hostel to see my dad and mom.

On seeing them I had tears of joy running down my cheeks. I packed up my belongings within an hour. I was excited to quit that hellhole.

I took my father's mobile phone and took some pictures of my hostel and the places where I used to study. I thanked some of the teachers who had helped me. We then started to Thanjavur in taxi from Namakkal. As I was getting away from my school, I remembered all the moments that had tested all my emotions in that place. And unlike cricket, if I had not achieved my desired result, then this would be the final visit to Namakkal.

CHAPTER TWENTY-THREE

OASIS

It would be injustice if I failed to narrate how I felt when it was all over. As I came out of the hostel my vision immediately turned colorful. Everything that happened around me seemed to be in slow motion.

I was able to distinctly notice birds flocking together in beautiful patterns, the different shapes of the clouds, the leaves in trees moving in the breeze as if bidding adieu for the last time.

The whole world around me looked a new.

Like a newborn baby watching the sky for the first time, I looked at the many pretty things in the place that I had lived for the last two years in. Namakkal was a hilly area with a lot of lakes and farmland. On our way back, I asked my father to take some pictures of me amongst the nature.

When we entered Thanjavur border, saw a board with the words, "Welcome to Thanjavur" I was very happy. A thousand words won't be enough to explain the joy that I felt at that moment.

I had dreamt a long time to experience that happiness and when I did, I felt sad for all those who had to leave their native town and work in distant cities and countries.

Thanjavur was adored as the rice bowl of Tamil Nadu. all over the district was filled with paddy fields. As we came near our home, I saw the Kittu ground.

I asked my father to drop me there and told him that I would return home after spending few hours in my favorite place in the city.

There was no one in the ground at that time. I had never seen the ground so empty. Even during exam time in our school days, getting the side pitch would be difficult.

As I walked up to the nets, I remembered all the practice matches and the bet matches that I had played there.

I then sat down on the ground despite the hot sun for some time. I felt at home in that ground . The people who crossed the roads looked at me quizzically. Obviously they must have considered me a mentally challenged teen for what a sane person dressed in decent clothes.

After two years of having survived on organic stuff that was called 'food' at my hostel, the *dosa* and the onion chutney prepared by mother tasted like ambrosia. I ate about ten *dosas* ,boneless chicken 65 and took my 16-hour nap to finally let out the mental and physical tiredness

Most of my school friends were checking their answers written in the exams and were calculating their scores for cut-off marks. I decided to do nothing regarding this kind of calculation. I focused on nurturing my health back while waiting for the results.

I googled about Yuvraj Singh and got to know that he had recovered completely from cancer and had been discharged from Boston hospital. I went to my favourite temple the same day, lighted a diya and thanked God for having helped him to recover from his illness.

I also pleaded with God to make Yuvraj fit enough to play for India again. I also prayed God to give me a chance to meet him once atleast in my lifetime. Amidst of everything happening around me, I felt like I had achieved something that day.

The thought that repeated was, I would be able to see my Yuvraj for the rest of my life which itself would be a huge gift for me. Just as I had prayed, he joined in the national team, practiced, soon after he got the Arjuna award.

A few days later, I met my old school friends from Maxwell, Don Bosco and from KV schools.

Among them, Vaithee and Dharma helped me to start a Facebook account and explained how it worked. The first name I searched was 'Pooja'my KV school sweety.

There were hundreds of Pooja in the Facebook and I didn't know how to find the Pooja that I was looking for.

In the spur of the moment, I gave a request to every one of those Poojas and started checking my account every morning as soon as I woke up to see how many had responded. The number never crossed zero for a long time.

One day I met Santosh raja, my old KV schoolmate, who gave me the actual ID of the Pooja to whom I had immediately sent a friend request. I continuously kept checking day and night for aher response. She finally accepted my request the following day. I was ecstatic and sent a "Hi" to her chat box.

My heart started pumping fast as I started sweating. She took one day to reply " Hi". To say I was over the moon in joy would be an understatement. I narrated the whole story from the day I met her till that moment and successfully told her that I had a crush on her.

To even my own surprise, she was impressed when she heard about the things I had done for her. But that the relationship never turned into a commitment as we both understood that it was just an infactuation and to this day we remain, good friends.

I have to thank Mark Zuckerberg for having given me a chance to let out my feelings and emotions without having the risk of public humiliation.

Amidst these memorable days, there were few terrible nights. I had nightmares where I dreamt of still being stuck in the Namakkal school, writing exams and woke up screaming out aloud believing that I left a question unanswered. I would lay upon my bed exhausted from the sheer terror that I still carried from the school.

CHAPTER TWENTY-FOUR

RESULTS

The day ,that my entire family awaited finally came. Yes! It was the day of the results. I went to the browsing centre to check the results. Meanwhile, my aunt had already seen the results and had called my grandpa who in turn rang me. I braced myself as he started reading out my marks.

English – 192/200
Tamil – 190/200
Maths -184/200
Physics-190/200

The world shattered around me and I felt weak in the knees when I heard "Physics 190". All my hopes of getting into a good medical college were swept away. I had lost 2.5 cut-off marks in Physics.

While he continued,

Chemistry- 199/200
Biology – 199/200

Total marks – 1154/1200 which is 96%

Only then I smiled. I calculated my medical cut off as 196.75 out of 200. My entire family was happy about my marks but I couldn't. I was short of 1 mark in my medical cut off. About the engineering cut off, the less said the better. I knew that with my current medical and engineering cut off it would not be of much use.

I wished to know where I had lost marks and hence applied for a copy of my answer papers. Once I got the photocopy of the Physics answer sheet, I noticed that I had lost 6 marks in a ten mark question as I had failed to write a vowel in an equation in a hurry. I had missed out on "a^2" in the three step and that was the reason for loosing these marks. Never in my dream did I expect that a small mistake such as missing out an "a^2" would change my life. But it wasn't the first time I had written like that. As I checked my old model exam answer sheets, I had done the same. My physics teacher had never corrected it and if he had, *probably*, I would've scored a 198.25 cut off and would've acquired an MBBS seat at Thanjavur government medical college. If only he had corrected properly , my life would have been so much easier. *If only....*

I became dejected soon as I realized that I could get medical seat only in a private medical college that too in self finance section with my cut off mark. As I came home my parents cheered me up saying that the medical cut off would not be high as always due to the tough Physics paper.

As we waited for the rank list, I was surprised to see myself at 1790 out of 2250 seats. It sprouted hope that I could get into a government college because there were 300 extra seats when compared to 2011.

Very soon the medical counseling was started and the open quota was finished first, followed by the seats for the

Backward caste which ended at 197.5 cut off mark and rest of the government seats went for candidates belonging to other reserved castes and I am not very much aware about reservations, only thing I know was, I belong to a Backward caste.

My only chance was, seat in a self-financing medical college where the fees would be about 5 lakh rupees per year. While most of my friends took seats in self-financing colleges owing to their wealthy background, I knew my family could never afford it. My mom tried to boost me saying that we could avail bank loan, but I told my father, "I don't want to trouble you anymore for my studies dad. I study Engineering."

Without knowing what to decide, we waited. I was surprised, that many of my Namakkal school mates took seats in government medical colleges in that Counseling.

A boy belonging to the BC category having the same cut off of 196.75 like me had got seat in a Government Medical College. I curiously asked him how he was able to get the seat. He said that there was a specific quota for his religion within the BC category.

I was puzzled at the revelation of reservation for a particular religion within the already existing reserved quota.

I thought reservation was based only on caste. Like this wasn't shocking enough, there was another boy from my school who also belonged to my caste and with the same cut-off had taken a seat in another government medical college. He told me that he changed his caste certificate from BC to DNC so as to avail the specific quota of MBC. I was astonished when I realised that the boy's father took up measures to change his community from Backward Caste to Most Backward just by changing the address proof so that he wouldn't miss a chance on getting into a government college.

I prodded on and asked him how he got to know it all. He said that one of his cousins had already lost the same place two years back. And to avoid the same fate, his father got him a new community certificate. Out of my curiosity, I asked my father "Why didn't you get me a new community certificate?" My father patted my back and smiled at me.

The day held far more surprises than I had anticipated. We all had the same opportunities, the same education and I had put in a lot of efforts than most of them. The worst part was that the parents of the students who acquired falsified certificates earned more than my father. Their actions were a true betrayal to people whom the reservation would be most beneficial.

I saw Swathish at the venue in medical counseling with cutoff 195.5 and he too lost the chance of getting a government seat in MBC quota. It was impossible for him to even imagine joining self finance colleges. Surprised about his marks because he studied in a Government school in Thanjavur, his father expired when he was studying for the 12th exams despite of that tragedy he struggled to score good marks,

It wouldn't bother me so much if seat was given to student like Swathish because he deserved the reservation even though his cutoff was low compared to mine after fighting those tough conditions in which he lived. But that was not the case here. My schoolmate from Green Park had studied what I had studied and had eaten what I had eaten but were able to get a seat in a government medical college with a cut-off lower than mine.

I stood in the middle of the road with no destination to travel to. All those hours of extra effort that I put in for obtaining this extra cutoff when others were enjoying and sleeping did not amount for anything. After that I understood that while fixing ambition, one have to learn about all the ladders and chutes in that path.

2012 year Tamilnadu Government Medical college cuttoffs

OC – 198.5
BC – 197.25
BCM – 196.25
MBC – 195.25

Is life a lie ?
Is pain the only end ?

This emptiness is not going to leave
Will this little bird get a wing?
Will this bird rise and fly ?
Will this bird touch its dream ?

Do all these emotions, feelings
just go in vain ?

Is the reality just repeated struggles and failures?
-Poet.Vivek

CHAPTER TWENTY-FIVE

WEAR UP

As I tried to recover from the second tragedy of my life, I decided not to work hard here after and stress myself over things that I couldn't control. I decided to go with the flow of life and be content though there were people willing to work hard for appearing in the National Medical Entrance Exam.

As I readied myself to let go of my dream, I was left with one choice alone – Engineering, which was the fancy choice of all 90's kids that time. I already know about the national level famous Deemed University situated near to my town, which was said to have 100 per cent transparency in filling the seats with no reservation. Counselling was also purely based on total marks and not by Engineering cut off, which came as an advantage for me.

Around that time, I happened to watch a movie "Enemy of the state" which inspired me to opt for the ECE department which was the best in that college. Intrigued to know more, my father and I set out to visit the college.

As I entered the campus.I was impressed by the campus environment. I soon became convinced that this is where my future would be shaped.

Even as the days passed, I was still caught up with the recent collapse of my childhood ambition. Despite trying to be happy, I failed miserably and couldn't sleep properly. On noticing my distress my father was dejected.

In order to help me open up,he took me to a hotel, The first question out of his mouth was, "Why are you not satisfied with your life?" I explained all that was pent up inside me.

He then said, "If this is your problem, have you ever imagined the story of my life or the people around the world? You see in Somalia, people suffer to get proper food, in Israel people suffer to live with their family. But you now have food, a roof on top of your head, a family that loves you and the freedom to dream. This was not the case when I was growing up. My mother died in a train accident, when I was in my undergraduation. I couldn't believe that she was no more, I lost myself along with her that day."

"I couldn't overcome the grief even after many months had passed. My mother was the one I loved the most and now she was also gone. There was no one to help me. But life had to go on. I motivated myself and ran a monthly handwritten magazine called "*Sigaram*" and its success helped me to move further. As I finished BSc Chemistry, I asked permission to do MSc. My father advised me to go to work as he couldn't afford money for my higher studies. I was adamant about post graduation. I had no choice, so I fought with my father and left the house and stayed with a friend.

'When I was looking for a way out of this predicament, a professor suggested that I should meet the chairman of that college. Sometimes it is indeed true when people say that God comes to us to give opportunities in the human form. In my case, it was Thulasi Ayyah Vandayar, the Chairman of the Sri Pushpam College in our city. He understood my situation and allowed me to stay with him. He promised that he would take care of my education. He never knew me before but helped me out of his benevolence.

'It was a once in the lifetime opportunity and I used it to the fullest. I successfully completed my MSc and immediately got a temporary posting in the Chemistry department of the same college as a lecturer. People told me that itself was a great achievement. But I did not stop there. I had to get into the permanent posting to get the Government salary as it was an Autonomous college.

I stayed loyal and straight forward to both my chairman and my job. Being straight forward did cost me many things. Some other corrupted people who did not like my straight forwardness made me to wait a long time for permanent posting.'I struggled for the next two years. Later in 1993, I married your mother. Again they left me out of the promotion list in the year you were born. I couldn't afford to spend time with you or to buy any good quality products due to my financial condition. And it was your Maternal uncle who helped us during that time.

'I took up tuitions and coaching classes to run our family and this took most of my day. When I came at night, you would be deep in sleep. And I would leave even before you woke up. I had no time to spend with my family or for myself but I never complained. This routine went on for more than two years and there seemed to be no end in sight for the vengeance the higher officials had for my sincerity. I quit the job and applied for the position of a government school teacher and started working there by 1997.

'For three years, I was at peace and was able to spend some time with my family. When I got a call from my chairman as a surprise he informed me that I was posted as a Permanent Chemistry professor in the year 2000. After having been patient for 12 years, I finally was able to achieve it. But if I were given a chance 10 or 11 years ago, I would have been in a position to put you in a self-finance medical seat.

'After that, your mother got a teaching job in a private school and that's how we were able to bring you up and give you all that you needed. After having suffered most of my life, there were moments when I wanted to give up everything. But I never stopped running as I knew this life was given to me by my chairman. In a world surrounded by money hungry educationalists, he offered free education being an open-minded person. I was not the only one as he had previously helped thousands of people in Thanjavur.

'All I am asking you is to be content. You have good parents to provide everything you need. A good university to study. So start enjoying your life because this is the life many dream of having."

I was able to understand what he said next and yet it came as a surprise to me. He told me "Do not follow my footsteps of being a straight forward person. You ought to be a little tricky to save yourself a place in this devious world. I know you have an eye on a Nobel prize since your childhood, there are some simple science facts left undiscovered. Take the opportunity which may be waiting to take you to success." These words of my father helped me realize so many things and motivated me to become the best in my chosen field.

That night after we had finished up, I understood that life was too short to have sorrows. I slept eagerly waiting for the next day as my attitude towards life had shifted dramatically.

Move forward
Courage is the only companion
Failures and injuries sculpts you
After the chisel hits the rock
It drops and gets shattered
The eyes of that sculpture won't shed tears for the departed shards.

If time brought thousand obstacles infront of you
When thousand lies try to pull you back
Move forward and face it.

If you stand at a distance and think
Even pond looks too deep for you
If you intend to step in
even sea will befriend you

Never always blame the fate
Blame yourself
Let the god get some sleep
You just try to find the reason for your life
- Poet Madhan karki

CHAPTER TWENTY-SIX

GET GOING

I was gnawed by the nightmares that continued even after having left that horrific place. I dreamt about writing the Physics exam again and I would jump out of my bed at 4 AM. I would immediately turn around and only when I realized that I was safe at home would go back to sleep.

Right at that moment, I was so happy to be back home. I was happy that I could sleep an extra three hours every day and there would be no study whistles anymore in my life. I was happy that I could do anything that I pleased.

With this mindset, I set off to begin the new chapter at Sastra University.

I was allocated to 'Z' section for the first semester which has students from different departments combined together as they all followed the same syllabus.

Over the years, I had developed a character trait of being a backbencher. As I sat there, the seat next to me was occupied by a leanfreaky guy with a funk. He told me he was Shivlal from Trichy. He was a day scholar.

When I answered his query regarding my 12th mark, he jumped three benches to the front. I understood that he misunderstood me as a studious guy

When he thought he was escaping me, he got caught with an even bigger nerd, the CBSE topper Power star Srinivasan. He quickly realized that a known devil was better than unknown angel and so he jumped back again to my bench.

The next day a soft-spoken guy named Sudharshan sat next to us, and we became friends within a week. The three of us were so alike that we never listened to classes but seriously discussed movies.

There were times when I knew straight up that I did not belong there. It was especially during the practical lab when I had to wear a Khaki uniform but I wanted to wear a white coat.

In the end, I would console and pat myself saying that I looked better in the khaki uniform.

The friends who had studied with me in Namakkal were posting photos on their Facebook . They were wearing their white coats , their stethoscopes and wrote cringey captions like

'God can't be every where so he sends Doctors.'

'Stethescope is not just an instrument but it is my Jewellery'

" Dr" not just my prefix but it is my super power.'

I would be upset on seeing these photos. Here I was with a cut off 196.75 and wearing khakhis whereas those who had lesser marks than me were going around in white coats only because they were able to buy their way into the medical profession.

Our favourite past time was to roam around the college to spot the beautiful girls in all the other departments. Shiva had a huge number of female friends including those who were fellow day scholars. Many girls would come around to talk to him and I would stand there having no clue about what move to make.

None of my school friends were in touch with me as I had left school by 10th grade. But to my surprise, I soon came to know that a few of my KV friends were in a different department of the college I couldn't meet them often and so my only company were - Shivlal and Sudharshan.

Shiva had a crush on one of our classmates and he took up the duty of stalking her. Whereas for me, having been in an environment surrounded by boys, speaking to girls by itself came as a huge struggle.

When Shiva realized this, he would crack up every time a girl crossed me. Nevertheless, he became my mentor and taught me how to start a conversation with girls.

After about a week, a girl named Gayatri from our class asked some sort of help to Shiva. She then soon joined our gang with her friends Ranjani and Ragavi.

We together started bunking classes and hanging out. Meanwhile, Shiva's description of his crush bored us out of our heads.

In the end, his crush had accepted his admission of liking her which pushed us all into a state of shock. It was surprising since we had never believed in that events would take such a quick turn for the good.

That first semester happened to be the most beautiful six months of my life. We grew closer to each other and enjoyed college to the fullest where we created our bucket lists. My friends understood everything that had happened in my life and how that had led to me to stop dreaming about things.

By then, they all unanimously decided that an understanding partner would help me to dream again. They constantly started looking out for girls compatible to my character.

It all first started with the task of me having to talk to a random girl. Most of the times, the girls would simply get angry and I would immediately point out that it was a game of truth or dare.

After a point, I started growing jealous of the good looking boys. I believed that because I was average looking guy, no girl would ever fall in love with me as they were almost already taken by the handsome ones.

As the routine went on, cricket came into my life once again. The selection criteria of the college cricket team were announced. I knew I did not want that lie anymore about cricket not being in my life but my love for the game was stronger than the dejected feeling inside me.

I then decided that if I were to go to the selections, I would do it with zero expectations.

Eventually, when the results came, it was an expected one. I got into the college team but nothing else was different. The seniors still played important matches and were dominant. But I took this opportunity purely to keep me in shape and keep me occupied with a hobby as I had stopped worrying about my cricket life.

Before we knew it, unit tests started and Gayatri helped us out during exams. We ended not studying at all whenever we gathered for group studies, Despite all this, when I did try and study, I struggled immensely with the maths papers.

On seeing this, my mom asked me to start preparing for the National entrance tests so I could try MBBS the next year. That suggestion brought back all the bitter memories that I had experienced due to the reservation system and shouted at her for bringing the topic over again.

I also told my parents that the MBBS chapter in my life was over and I was satisfied with engineering.

I knew I could never pass engineering without understanding the basic concepts, and so Shiva and I took up other methods. We prepared cheatsheets from Gayatri's notes to pass the exam.

That was pretty much how we successfully finished the first unit test.

CHAPTER TWENTY-SEVEN

EXCITEMENT

My mom took me to a famous astrologer (Naadi Jothidar) who was an "expert" in predicting a person's future based on their thumbprint and palm creases. As soon as I gave my thumbprint, I waited eagerly for him to predict my future.He touched the wrong nerve right off the bat.

He said, "According to this palm script your son must be in the field of '*Oudatham*' which refers to Medicine. Is he a doctor?" He then talked about many things that he could predict from the palm script such that my marriage was an arranged marriage.

The last point got my attention and I asked him if there was any chance for me to have a love marriage. My parents gave me a weird look. He told me that I would definitely have an arranged marriage and laid down the fact that I did not stand any chance with love. That demotivated me from all the dreams about love stories that I had imagined after growing up on the romantic movies of Director Gowtham Menon. I was determined to prove him wrong and sincerely believed that my hope could overcome the predictions of any soothsayer.

Never did I know that my dreams could manifest themselves in the form of Malavika, who was a day scholar.

Shivlal had asked me to speak to her. I thought about all the reasons I could come up with to avoid a direct conversation and so finally said that I could do better over the phone if I could get my hands on her number. Shiva then let out an exaggerated laugh. He challenged me to make her become my girlfriend and wrote down her contact number on my hand.

In spite of my prelimary shock on how he had her number, I took it. The next morning I sent her a 'Hi'. As the conversation began after she replied, we talked about our likes and dislikes, families and addresses. She kept asking a lot of questions to know all the details about me. Just as I thought I could speak to her in person the next day, I got a call from her number and imagined she was calling to say that she liked me.

I picked up the call only to realize that it was her mother on the other side. Her mother had called to warn me and asked me to study properly and advised me not to involve myself with her daughter. She was the one whom I have chatted whole day.

I got tensed and immediately switched off my phone. I went directly to Shiva's house and started strangulating him asking him why he gave the contact number of Malavika's mother. He explained that he did not know her mother was using the same mobile. I was all the more scared as I had shared everything about me including my address. I was scared of what my father would do if it were ever to reach his ears.

As I switched on the mobile the next day, I received a text that read "Good night" from her mother's number. I was puzzled on why, how and who sent that. When I informed this on my way to college. I hit Shiva black and blue when he made such things up as he had been the sole reason for all the chaos. My crush started and ended before an entire day had passed.

During the lunch break, Malavika had come to our class and on seeing her I lost myself. She asked Gayatri "Where is Shreedher?". Gayatri turned to my side and I signaled her not to point me out. She understood that and I told her that shreedher was absent, referring myself in the third person. On hearing that, she left. Malavika was determined to find me out. She made it a routine to come to my class every day during lunch and I would hide under my desk. After a few days, she left me alone and I eventually forgot that incident altogether.

We all knew that Shiva was a ardent fan of watching movies. He had always wanted to do a short film and I insistently kept requesting him to give me a character in his story. He never heeded my request. He would only want me when there was work to be done with the script. We always crept up to the terrace of one of the buildings in my college hostel for all our group discussions and to put it simply it was like heaven on the earth for us boys.

Some smoked and drank while others played the guitar and sang songs as they enjoyed the nights with gossips and talks. A few of them would be flirting with their crushes and finally us – the group of 5 – would be discussing a short film script.

The script would start with a scene that changed to a different position in the story as the discussion progressed which would turn out to be unrelated when we finally finished. Then as we all finally agree to one plot and narrate it to someone, they would say that some Korean or Japanese movie had the same plot. I soon realized that it was not a easy task to come up with original story and wondered how movie directors come with so many of them.

I also wondered how much creativity was needed in writing a story, editing it followed by choosing the right music and the all other things needed to bring the magic of making a scene perfect. I felt those with a creative mind were indeed gifted by God.

One day, when I boarded the bus to go home, one of my bus mates told me that her friend liked my silver chain and braceletthat I wore. As I asked who it was, she pointed out the girl. It was all flowers showered on my hearts when I saw her. There were no words to explain how beautiful she was.

My eyes wanted to see her forever. Her name was Abinaya. After a long time, I wanted to do something worthwhile in my life again. I wanted to speak to her. I decided to come to college regularly to see her every day.

CHAPTER TWENTY-EIGHT

FIRST LOVE

As soon as I realized I liked her, I gathered all information about her from my KV schoolmate Raja who was in her class.

"Her name is Abinaya, IT department. She is from Kalpakam. Both her parents were government servants and she had a younger brother who was in his 10th grade". Everyone I spoke to said that she had a good character and a decent sense of fashion. In college, she always go with with her gang of five girls.

I also learnt that she never spoke to unknown boys. She had received three love proposals in this college and she had rejected all of them. One of those who tried to flirt with her was a senior from the Mechanical department. I deduced that it would be difficult to make her my girlfriend.

I stumbled upon chance to speak her . I sent her a Facebook request. Life after that was a whole new experience, it became a mandatory practise for me to go to the IT department every day and talk to Raja as an excuse to get a good look at her. This went on for a while and I knew that I had to move quickly before someone else approached her.

I sought out Shiva's help to start a conversation with her. He took me to the IT department and asked me to stand in a spot,I asked him "what is the Plan?". He then went near Abinaya and shouted that "That boy wants to speak with you" pointing at me and walked away.

She turned and looked straight into my eyes and for a moment I lost myself and stood frozen like a statue.

I couldn't bring myself to even say 'hello' and so she left me with a blank look. I was furious with him for landing me in an awkward situation and in a fit of rage, I started beating up Shiva asking him why he would take me there without any plan.

He explained, "This is the right chance for you to speak to her again. When you see her tomorrow, tell her that you are sorry for what I did and start a conversation from that point."

I let him go from my tight clench and thanked him for having given me an actual idea this time.

The next day when I saw her, I told her how sorry I was for what my friend had done. She brushed off that incident. As she said this, I saw her blue eyes and stood mesmerized.

Shiva's taunted me for having wasted the one good opportunity I had with her. He told me to try again in asking her to accept my request on Facebook so we could atleast chat virtually.

The next day I saw Abinaya walking with her friend towards the canteen and I followed them. I was waiting for the right opportunity to talk to her. As soon as I approached her, she went to the counter to place her order.

I stood there not able to look at her friend,she gave me a weird look that said anyway I am going to get a insult so I bend down looked at the *Channa* masala at their table which her friend was eating with keen interest and I was thinking how to start my convo with Abinaya.

As soon as Abinaya came back and saw me starring at the food plate ,she sarcastically asked me to eat it if I was hungry.

I told her that I wanted to talk to her. I said, "I am Shreedher from the ECE department. I have been trying to talk to you for quite some time now. I am planning on directing a short film and you look just perfect for my script. I just wanted to know if you are interested in acting."

She said, "I'm sorry. My parents will not allow that."

"That's okay. But if you are interested please contact me anytime" I said and left the spot immediately.

I was beyond happy when I had finally spoken to her and was even more delighted when she accepted my Facebook request that very day. I even gave my gang a treat to celebrate that beautiful moment.

I continued to see her every day and it soon came to my knowledge that the senior guy from the Mechanical department had been openly stalking her and forcing her to get into a relationship with him. This act was simply unacceptable. I wanted to beat that senior to make him come back to his senses.

When I told this to Shiva, he laid down the options for me. He said, "If you hit that senior boy you might as well become a person of interest and fear in the college. That is because generally the Mechanical department boys tend to show off their macho and are considered as the thugs of the college.

If a guy from the Electrical department beats him up, it would lead to a better rivalry. But again, if he were to beat you up, you might as well get the sympathy from Abinaya and it will come in handy when you try to impress her. It is a win-win situation"

I heeded his advice and got ready for 'The Fight of the Generation' the likes of which the college had ever seen. I voluntarily went up to the senior and started a conversation which then became a heated argument. But before we could lay hands on each other, people around us came in between and separated us.

Evidently, the news had reached Abinaya and she texted me in Facebook pleading with me never to involve myself in fights again. She also said that she would take care of the situation with the senior boy. I couldn't understand why she was trying to stop me and asked her the same.

Her answer came as a drug that took me past the proverbial ninth cloud. She said, "I don't want you to get into trouble. I say so because you are one who is close to me and I care for you and not the other guy ".

What would you want other than to hear his crush say that she cared for you? With that, we became good friends. Now I realized that she liked not only my chain andbracelet but also the person who was wearing them. Shiva told me that it might be the right time for me to go profess my true feelings towards her.

Since I did not want to rush things, I waited for the right situation.

Our conversations became interesting with each passing day. I once played *'Mundhinam parthane'* song on my keyboard and sent her the video in FB. To my surprise, she told me that she liked it very much. Then with the black guitar gifted by my father, I wanted to participate in that year's inter college cultural.

Soon I began practising by watching the performances of famous guitarists and video tutorials from YouTube.

A lean and a long-haired guy wearing a leather jacket closed his eyes, strummed a single chord and the entire crowd went crazy as they roared for every other chord he played. I had goosebumps by the time he finished his song and imagined myself on that very stage someday.

College was fun and on one of those days, we bunked classes to go to a movie '*Pizza*' suggested by Shiva. We planned to go for the 11 AM show but unfortunately, that show ran house full in almost all the theatres. How a movie with a debut actor could attract such a large audience on a weekday, I wondered ! Shiva explained, "Though the hero Vijay Sethupathi is new he has good acting skills.

He has acted in many short films and a feature film '*Thenmerku Paruva Katru*' that got a National award in 2010. Besides the technical team has director Karthik Subburaj, producer CV Kumar and music composer Santhosh Narayan.

This pretty much evolved as the dream team that is going to rule the cinema industry in the near future." I was amazed at the knowledge Shiva had about cinema.

We finally went to the 2 p.m show. I was awestruck by the hero's acting skills the script and the music. It came across as an astonishing film with a concept and screenplay very unique to the Tamil film industry.

After watching that story I wanted to try directing a short film and started to write a story called '*True caller*'. As I narrated the story to my gang and the hostellers, they gave me a good response and supported me in directing that script. But I knew there was so much that I had to learn about direction and so planned to start with that. After cricket and MBBS, script writing attracted me.

Since I had nothing to loose in this, I started developing my skills in this as I knew that my career in engineering was always a big question.

After three months, the long-awaited GVM movie '*Neethane En Pon Vasantham*' was released and all the boys in the hostel pooled enough money to book the theatre for a private screening just for them. Almost every one of us had a celebrity crush on the movie's female lead Samantha. Thus it was natural that we all went for the first day first show.

I started relating everything in the movie to Abinaya and myself. I even took notes from the film and wrote a letter in romantic way to convey my feelings. But Shiva suggested, " It would be best to tell her in person rather than by a letter. Also never ask her to be your friend in case she did not accept you as her lover because you will have to fake your love for her friendship."

I accepted his suggestion and I began to practice my love proposal speech with my hostel mates.

CHAPTER TWENTY-NINE

HOSTEL STORIES

As I went to the hostel, the stories poured in. I heard stories of love that were so pleasant to a point where I was brimming with jealousy. Some guys told about their relationships which began when they were in 11th and 12th grades while I was suffering in a hell hole during that same time. They had opportunities like freedom to speak to girls at school, at tuition classes, at family functions and decked in their best while I had to wait for months end even to meet my parents. Sudharshan suggested, "Loving a girl in life and marrying the same is a gift." On hearing these the colourful flowers of marriage life blossomed in my heart.

I also happened to hear stories of betrayal and cheating in relationships. I even got a metaphorical heart attack when I heard the story of a girl who had a secret affair with her best friend which she deliberately hid from her boyfriend. Eventually, the boyfriend learnt about in an ugly way. The girl broke up with him at ease and got into a relationship with her best friend. That truly shook up my imagination of relationships always ending on a happy note.

I also learnt that breakups do not happen only due to parental pressure and their strict measures but also due to....Possessivene of a lover ,no reason for breakup, boys in this class, fall into the habit of drinks and drugs in order to forget the lady love who broke up with them.I could also see that no one was ready to sacrifice one's own time for their beloved partner.

But I understood from having watched my parent's relationship that a relationship could survive only if we could adjust and try to keep ourselves in tune with the changes around us.

These stories helped me to change my outlook of relationships. I learnt that love has the ability to raise people to great height but at the same time it can also push to down deep wells with no hope of coming back up.

The relationship between my mother and father taught me that flexibility, stability and faith are paramount for a couple to be happy. Every relationship would face its share of problems and those who were ready to face can succeed it. It didn't escape my notice that many in my generation saw relationships as a way to gratify their lust .

I thought that it was not the right time for experimenting with relationships as I had faced enough shortcomings in life. I just wanted to spend time having fun and so I decided to postpone my plans of proposing love to next year after successfully completing my first year in this college.

As the first semester was around the corner, Shiva and I crept into the hostel for the entirety of the exam days for our so-called group study. We ended up having lots of fun. But where is the fun if we did not get into trouble? One night at around 10 PM my stomach started aching due to ulcer pain and to my plight, no one had any snacks in their rooms. So I had to go outside and on my way back after buying biscuits, the watchman caught me. He immediately called and informed the warden. He then gave me the phone to talk to the warden. I did not know how to resolve the situation. I decided to I improvise on the spot.

"Hello?" said a gruff voice from the other end.

"Hello" said I.

"What is your name? What are doing out at this time??"

"My name is Srinivasan sir, I went outside to get some biscuits due to my ulcer pain."

"Don't you know the hostel rules? You should have done this before 9 PM."

"Sorry sir, I never expected this."

"Okay. What is your room number?"

"Room no. 333, Sir."

"Let this be the last warning. Come to my office and hand over an apology letter to me tomorrow."

"Okay, sir. Thank you."

Next day I submitted an apology letter at the warden's room without him or the real Srinivasan knowing that.. Finally, we finished the semester exams successfully and we boarded a train to Kerala without any plans. We stayed at random places and enjoyed our time to the fullest.

As soon as the vacation neared its end, the results came. I had gotten a CGP (cumulative Grade point) of 6.7out of 10 in that semester. The CGP played an important role in the campus interview where the companies always chose the candidates with a good CGP. The ECE students always had low CGP scores as the examiners who corrected our papers were strict.

As we moved on to the second semester, my entire gang was shuffled to different sections. I went to the 'T' section. I missed the presence of my friends and our friendly banter. So from meeting in person as a group, we began talking in a Whatsapp group. I started feeling alone again, as it was a whole new class and I used to bunk college to go to the

Big temple in Thanjavur. I used to sit on a stone bench listening to Yuvan songs. As I grew up in Thanjavur, I had gone to the temple numerous times but never I had ever taken the effort to admire the massive structure that was built thousand years back. I spent time to know about the history of the colossal structure and was soon surprised by the detailed planning and efforts that went into each step of this massive undertaking. I realised that there were many of my generation who did not know about these too. I wanted people to know about the temple and the history of the Chola dynasty who built it.

I started writing a feature film script with an idea of Kamal Hassan and Vijaysethupathi as the protagonists based on historical facts mixed with fictional elements. I was determined to write such a script that when it was made as a movie it should make everyone to astonish about Cholas and bring them to Thanjavur to see the temple they had constructed.

As I completed the script, I narrated the story to my gang and just as I had dreamt, they were both shocked and surprised. By the end, they were completely baffled that they did not believe or accept the fact that I had written the script. (Later that very script turned out to be my first Novel "CODED TRIANGLES" which I released in 2019 which was a huge hit).

As I moved to the 'T' section, I immediately spotted Malavika. As soon as the professor walked in and called Shreedher Priyan while taking attendance, I raised my hand. She recognized me instantly . I thought she would come up to me and burst out. Before she could speak , I said, "Sorry for what I did. Why have you been asking for me from the last semester?"

She explained that her mother had sent the 'Good night' message to me by mistake and that she had searched for me just so she could explain the situation. I felt stupid for having avoided her and we both laughed it away. We soon became good friends.

I settled in my new class in a few days. As Shiva's girlfriend was in the same class, he used to come whenever there was a break. Every evening our entire gang met in the lawn before we left home.

Academics was getting tougher and I felt maths to be the hardest. Since my childhood maths was always my villain in academics. To rectify the situation, Raja suggested group study at Mohan's house. The interesting fact was that three of us were poor at solving problems. So Raja arranged a Maths professor from our college to come home to take tuition for the M2 paper. We made a pact where we hid this from the world as we were embarrassed to take tuitions even after coming to college.

CHAPTER THIRTY

LOVE OR CRICKET

Staying at home after being in the hostel for the past two years was an opportunity to spend time with my family. Unfortunately one night, my mom had severe chest pain and I did not know what to do.

In panic, I rushed to the kitchen and brought back a glass of water which helped her settle down a little.

The only thing that ran through my head was if I have written that a^2 correctly in my physics exam then as a medical student I would have been in a position to know what should have been done during chest pain. The following day we went to the doctor and he told that the pain was due to an gastritis and that there was nothing to worry about.

There were instances when I learned that my mom was not happy with my life. She knew about my problems but she had always wanted the best for me.

She raised me with stories filled with morals and to believe in destiny. She taught me to pray to Godevery day as she believed prayers had a significant role in our lives.

My mother had struggled very hard by working in a privates schools to provide economy of our family. I felt guilty for not having satisfied her dream of seeing me as a doctor.

Many a time I pledged to make her proud and to take family responsibilities onto my shoulder. The time was nearing.

As the days were running , I got back to my life. Raja once called me to play cricket with a Tennis ball. A new team came in place with Avengers Srinivasan as our captain.

It was then that I got to know that Avengers Srini was also a day scholar who was playing in the Thanjavur district Nets.

He even asked me to participate in the under-19 selection. I said that I had enough from the nets and there was nothing more for me to prove.

I was very happy with tennis ball cricket and our new team was bowling out the other famous teams in our college. Raja, Srini and I gave all-round performances in all the matches and there was nothing more we could've expected.

The second semester was eventually got over and I finished it off with a 6.8 CGP successfully.

As I moved on to the second year, I geared up to propose my love to Abinaya. Before I went to her, Gayatri had asked me to check on her idea about relationships and her family situation.

As I studied everything about her, the situations seemed favourable to me.

I tried talking to her several times but I couldn't bring the courage. Gayatri then told me that she would inform me when the situation would be completely supportive of my efforts.

One Sunday morning, Srini called me. He told me that there was one last chance to still participate in the under-19 selection. I said I did not want to attend and hung up. But right after the call, I got nervous. I walked outside and as I saw my old Cricket shoes. It called me to wear it.

Then I got selected for Under 19 Thanjavur team and practice matches were held on Sundays. We were divided into two teams. Since I was a senior player there, I got a chance to lead one of the teams during a practice match. After winning the toss I chose to bowl.

It had been very long and my hunger for a good match had grown into a raging fire. I bowled a decent spell, giving 48 runs and taking 2 wickets in 10 overs. The target for us was to score 224 in 50 overs.

The opponents began their bowling attack with bowlers in top form who took wickets at regular intervals. The scoreboard showed 86 runs for 6 wickets in 33 overs.

Then it was my time to bat and I knew I had to play a captain's knock in order to save my team. I was under extreme pressure to take my team to a decent score since it was my first match as a captain.

I went to the crease with my heart thumping fast in my chest. The first ball was a full pace delivery. It felt a nudge in my bat and it went straight to the keeper. He missed it and the ball went for four. That was not a good start.

The slip started sledging me saying things like I wouldn't last the next two overs – the same statement that I had heard three years back in Karaikudi.

This touched my ego and I determined that this was the only chance to prove myself and to remove the guilt for having lost my wicket all those years ago.

While I started playing solid defensive strokes, there was a continuous fall of wickets at the other end. I calculated that the chance of winning was not great and so decided to take the match till the 50th over and giving a tough fight to the bowling side.

With every ball I faced, I repeated to myself one thing. "Watch the bowler's hand releasing the ball. Concentrate and play according to the length and the line with loose hands. Do not prejudge the shot."

I stayed on the pitch until the last over to the end with a team score of 151 for 9 wickets in 50 overs. Though I scored 16 runs from 64 balls, I stood till the end.

This helped me let go of my pent up guilt and gave me confidence of my cricketing skills. This is the beauty of cricket. It provided me an opportunity to stay calm and stick to a plan.

After having played well in that innings and having the advantage of being a senior player, I knew that I would get a chance in the first match of the state level tournament.

I packed my things once again for a Tournament in Theni. By luck, I caught a cottonseed which had previously been lucky to me at the railway station and expected for some magic to happen at the tournament in Theni.

Just as I had boarded the train, Gayathri called me and informed me that Abinaya's friends had gone home for the weekend and that Abinaya was alone at the hostel. She also informed me that if I came by noon of that day, I could meet her in her department alone and would be able to spend some time with her.

Right then, I couldn't decide if I wanted to go to Theni or to get down from the train for that once in a blue moon opportunity of talking with Abinaya.

My heart finally laid it down for me. It said: "*You have had enough chances in cricket and this time you have to go for Abinaya.*" And I listened to it.

I got down from the train at Trichy as I informed my team that I am not well. I took my kit bag and got on a bus to Thanjavur. I arrived at my university with my kit bag as I ran towards the IT department.

The second year students were conducting some program and Abinya was a part of it. I had reached around 11 AM and had to wait till 4 PM without having food or water, just to meet her.

Finally, as she came out, I went near her and looked straight in her eyes. Before I could even begin my conversation, she cut me off with, "Shreedher, I know your intentions. Do not follow me hereafter. I am not interested in whatever you are trying. So it would be better if you spend your time on improving your future."

Ok. So I left my spot in the district cricket team for this. Fine. But I was not going to go back without saying anything.

I told her I had one question. “Why are you not interested in me? Is there any particular reason?"

“I am asking you the same question. Should there be a particular reason for me to have interest in you? Have you done something special except for roaming behind a girl like a roadside Romeo?"

That did it. I decided that there was no use in trying my luck with her.

“Sorry, Abinaya. I will not disturb you hereafter", said I and left the place.

I called Gayatri and broke down as I told her what happened. I didn’t have strength in me to walk further. I sat at the canteen alone . Gayatri and Sudharshan rushed to me and consoled my broken heart.

But I couldn’t stop with my ranting. “What she said is correct. How can she possibly have interest over someone like me? Just like that umpire once said, no one knows about all the efforts of my life.

Who cares if I read biology and I scored 196.75 at the end. I was not a doctor. I was an engineer and my scoreboard is zero. I got rejected by cricket, I got rejected by medicine. Now to top it off, I was also rejected by Abinaya. I must have gotten used to rejection but my dumb heart just doesn't get it.

It never understood that I should not dream about anything and all my hopes will come back to disappoint me someday or other. And now there was nothing to dream about in my life."

Gayathri and Sudharshan did not want me to travel but I insisted that they dropped me at the bus stand. I came back to my house at night and told my parents that I did not feel good. I did not go to college for the next few days.

When I was on leave, Sudharshan called me and told me that Abinaya was in a relationship with a boy from her own department . My gang insisted that I should fight with her for having spoken in a harsh manner when I went to open up my feelings for her. Because if she had informed me that she was committed with someone , I would have left her alone without creating a scene.

I asked them to let it go. It would have been wrong on my part if I had done that as she never gave me false hopes nor did she try to cheat either me or her boyfriend.

Moreover, if she had told me she was in a committed relationship with another guy when I proposed to her, it would have only hurt me more. I would have ended up comparing myself to her boyfriend. Instead, she decently expressed her feelings that she had no interest in me and the next day she made me understand that she had a boyfriend. Even though I was hurt, I was not angry at her because she stayed true to everyone, including me.

My parents grasped my mood swings during the following days. So I avoided staying at home. The second-year unit tests started and I stayed in Power star srinivasan's room.

His roommates Pragadeesh, Sandeep and Adhithya taught me many of the engineering concepts only to stir up my fear. I did not want to take up my unit tests because I felt I would fail as the unit tests were usually tough.

After running so much the distance to run never decreased
After singing so much the song to be sung still continues
I am not able to understand anything
In total, nothing works well for me.

The world is running fast
My bike is punctured here
Even useless guys are teasing me
What is the role that God play here?

I turned out to be the Joker
I am riding inside a failure loops

I wandered alone in a beach
I cried in the middle of the road and torn out
I can't bear the burden,I am not a donkey.
I am looking for the switch of the fused bulb

I went to bed, in the middle of the night
I woke up and slept, woke up and slept
I cried and smiled, cried and smiled
I am traveling in boat and shore is not visible
- Poet Dhanush

As a routine, whenever I felt stuck in life, I would look at my Yuvraj Singh photo and every time it gave me hope. It reminded me of my hero who used to bounce back again and again. In spite of having faced so many downfalls, I still believed that there is something big will happen for me oneday.

When Yuvraj was rejected a spot in the international squad, he kept practicing hard and reclaimed his spot each time.

Following the footsteps of my favourite star, I waited for my good times. I did not have any more personal ambitions. My only dream was to see Yuvraj Singh playing in the Indian jersey again.

I developed a pastime of collecting trivia about Yuvraj Singh's achievements and quotes attributed to him.As I read his interviews and saw his post match conferences, I got a boost of confidence to take on the googly balls that life threw at me. He never accepted defeat. Neither did I.

CHAPTER THIRTY-ONE

Real Cotton Seed

As exams started once again, it was loathsome to study a few subjects such as Digital electronics, Maths, Signals and Systems. It felt being hit on the head with nails when I tried to understand them and yet I had to do it in order to pass through the rough road I was walking on.

The night before I had the exam on signals and systems, I was trying hard to solve some minimum number of problems till 3 a.m. just so I could move on to studying theory.

As time passed by. I realised that there was no hope left for me to pass. I closed the books and slept.

On the day of the exam, I went to the building were the Electronics department was located. Gayathri, Sudha, Shiva, Ranjani and Ragavi had come there for a final revision where Gayathri was summing up the important points.

The exam was scheduled at 1 p.m. and we raced to cover everything. I got a call from my mother around 11 a.m. As I attended it she told me that my dad and she were in Chennai for the medical counselling.

I said, “Stop joking mom. I have an exam. I will call you later.”

My mom then said, "We came to attend the medical counselling of this year with your last year cut off of 196.75. We wanted to check the possibility of getting a government seat. This time again the government colleges are all taken. But the self-finance college seats are available and I called you to ask if we can take the seat this time? Are you still interested in pursuing medicine?"Then I remembered that they got sign from me regarding this year medical counseling since same cutoff marks can be applied this year also in Tamilnadu medical counseling. Now they went to counseling with a permission letter to attend instead of me since I had my exams here.

My mind started calculating right away as I spoke into the phone. "Okay. So why is it that you are still thinking about getting me a self-finance seat? It costs about 5 lakhs per year and by the end of 5 years it will inflate to 30 lakhs. Did you think about how will we be able to pay that amount? I do not want a career that starts with such a huge debt. And to be honest, medicine is a 5.5-year course now.

Even if I were to join, it will be 6.5 years for me. People around me will laugh at me for not joining last year itself despite having a chance. Stop confusing me and yourself. I am satisfied with engineering. So come back to Thanjavur. Bye.” I hung up the call even before my mother could react.

In about a minute or so, I got a call from my grandmother.

“ Shreedher *kanna*, do not think too much about that MBBS seat. Money can be earned at any point but opportunities come once. In your case, it has come for a second time. If you do not use it properly this time, you might regret it later in life. A doctor’s job is equal to that of

God. I will sell my house. Once we do that your grandfather and I can move in with you.

I can contribute a few lakhs toward your education and the rest your father can pay by availing an education loan. If the money happens to be your only worry, there is no problem. This is the least we could do to help. When you become a successful doctor, buy me a bigger house than the one we sold. People will respect you not for the money you have or to the family you belong to but by the profession you are in."

"Grandma I understand everything. But I do not want you to sell the house. I know the time, tears and sweat that went into building that house. Also, I am satisfied with engineering and I am happy with what I am doing. Please grandma. Let us stop talking about medicine," I replied and hung up once again.

As my mother called me again, she said, "Shreedher, this is your last chance. Think before you say no."

"No. No. No. I don't want MBBS." I screamed into the phone, hung up and went to the exam hall.

As I sat at my desk and looked out the window, time seemed to slow down. Birds flew slowly and trees moved even slower. As the invigilator gave the answer sheet I wrote my roll number. To my surprise, I remembered my 12th public exam roll number better than the current one.

As I received the question paper, I realized I did not know the answer to a single question. At that moment, my entire past flashed in front of me.

Starting from the moment when my parents left me in the Namakkal residential school, my school's director assuring me that those two years would change my life, waking up for the study whistle at 5.30 AM every day for two years, adjusting to the most disgusting toilets and crazy psychos ever, jumping school compound wall at 4 AM to study, losing proper sleep due to all the construction noise. All these efforts were to make me a doctor.

Suddenly the invigilator pointed at my answer sheet and asked me, "Why are you sitting without writing the exam?" I tried to concentrate on the question paper but the past came rushing back once again. Finally, the words of the Umpire lodged in the corner of my mind popped up.

"Opportunity never comes according to our wish. We should grab any rope that is available instead of waiting for the right one."

I could see the rope waiting outside for me, eager to give me a second chance. And I wondered that I was too harsh in my decision. I gave back my blank answer sheet to the invigilator and ran out of the room to take my mobile from the bag.

I dialled my mother's number and asked her to take any available seat in any medical college. But I couldn't reach my mom. The rope seemed to be slowly slipping away.

I immediately called my father. As I heard the dial tone and no answer, I realized that my father was already inside the counselling room and that I might be a little too late.

I felt dejected at having lost another chance. My body felt numb and lifeless. On seeing me sitting at the road with no one around, a watchman pulled me up and asked me to sit in a stone bench.

I sat and watched the clouds in the sky. Thousands of thoughts rushed in a blur. But I prayed to God to do something about what I had done.

Just then, I got a call from my mother.

Even before she could say hello, I was shouting. "Mom please take any government quota self finance seat.. I do not know why I refused when you called me. I need this.

Please."

My mom laughed and said, "We have taken a government quota self finance seat at a private college in Madurai." You worked very hard to get this seat,many people not even have this opportunity to take this seat.

We can't afford a Management seat paying 50 lakhs of rupees as a donation but we can manage a government quota self finance seat to achieve your dream.

Tears rolled down my cheeks. I asked, "How did you take it when I asked you not to?"

"I am your mom. Every mom knows what her child wants. I know your life better than you. Though you said no I have always known what your heart wants. I knew you love medicine and that you always dreamt of becoming a doctor."

How my mom felt the same what I prayed to god, either god said to my mom or all mom's are the actual god I don't know,that's how I understood why mothers are cherished across time and cultures

Until that moment, I had never really felt of having achieved anything. As my gang came out after the exams, I hugged Shiva and Sudha as I informed them about the interesting turn of events that happened in the afternoon.

I told them that my family had decided to see me as a doctor despite the costs involved. My friends couldn't believe that I was going to turn into doctor from an engineer in just over three hours.

Even today, I think about how my grandparents had to struggle to buy their house. My parents struggle wasn't easy either. They had to undergo untold hardship to raise me and give me a decent life.

So for a middle class boy to become a doctor, it took two generations hard work. I had sucked their blood to become a doctor. Was it all worth it? Only time would tell.

Opportunity is like an angel. It will come at least once in your life.
If you respect it, you will keep seeing it again and again your life.
Show any disrespect and you will never see it again.
- Jigarthanda movie

CHAPTER THIRTY-TWO

TRIUMPH

2013

If there was one word to describe this part of my life it would be happiness.

From the day that I knew I would join medical college, I had imagined myself as a dashing guy who was well groomed, formally dressed with a white coat.

Yes! I found myself among 150 students gathered in a new building with highly furnished classrooms and centralized air conditioning.

I was living my dream as I stepped into that Medical College in Madurai. I happened to belong to the first batch of that college which was a sweet surprise. When I sat there amongst the crowd, as the dignitaries addressed the gathering, one thing kept running inside my mind.

"Shreedher, you know how much you longed to wear this white coat. Achieving one's dream does not come easy for anybody, here you are living the dream that came as a gift of your family's sacrifice and your patience. Let your scorecard be the tribute to all these when you walk out of this institution as Doctor Shreedher Priyan"

Apart from this, what would my life be without my superhero in it?

While I wore my White coat here in my medical college,my hero wore his Indian jersey again....

Yes! Yuvaraj Singh with number 12 in his jersey was finally back after all the turmoils and fit to play ODIs and T20s. His millions of fans had longed for this moment for the past two years.

Like my hero, I started the marathon again. I noticed my BC badge over my jersey once again and I was asked to run according to my caste. Even before we could pat ourselves for getting into MBBS, we were made to race for our PG entrance examinations. They informed us that a mere MBBS degree alone would not help us to go ahead much in our careers.I know no one in this world allow us to enjoy our present ,they always add future loads in our back but I never heard any of them I was completely enjoying my hard earned MBBS degree.

After the orientation, we gathered at our classroom, then met by Dr John, Physiology professor. He asked us to introduce ourselves and clarify any queries we had regarding the college.

Every one of them introduced themselves and asked basic doubts regarding the college's facilities, timetable, academics etc.

And then it was my turn. I stood up, "My name is Shreedher Priyan and I am from Thanjavur. I have one question, sir and by now you people know what my question would be "Can we start a college cricket team sir?"

And there it began,

CHAPTER THIRTY-THREE

Bachelor of cricket – Part 2

Score card of Bachelor of medicine – Coming soon......

Opportunity does not knock, it presents itself when you beat down the door.

1) Two years as a College Cricket Captain (2013-2015) – New ball bowler for my college team with more than 150 wickets and 8 half centuries with bat.

2) Three years as a Sports Secreatary (2013-2016) – Initiated sports in my College

3) Started photography page "PRIYANOGRAPH" in Facebook

4) Started You tube channel " Priyan 666" – Directed 5 short films

Velammal Medical College Hospital & Research Institute,

Reserach And Development Center

Completed research projects

NO	Name of the investigator	Title of the research
1.	K . Aravindan Guide Dr . M . Sarvanan	Comparison of visual reaction time between myopic and emmetropic subjects (ICMR APPROVED)
2.	Nethra S Guide Dr . Vaishnavi A	A Study on the level of stress and perceived coping strategies among medical students
3.	Surjeet Acharya Guide Dr . Anandjanagand	Spectrum of Dermatophytes causing taenia corporis and possible risk factors (ICMR APPORVED)
4.	N . Shreedher Priyan Guide Dr . BN Vallish	Prevalence of cardiovasclar risk factors in engineering and medical and students in Madurai, Tamil nadu (ICMR APPROVED)
5.	Prasanna Rajguru Guide Dr . R. Sudhakar	Comparison of platelets indices with platelet count to predict disease severity in seropositive Dengue cases (ICMR APPROVED)
6.	J. Anita Priyadarshini Guide Dr . A. Sangeetha	Prevalence and risk factors of non-alcoholic fatty liver disease in patients attending master health check-up in VMCH&RI (ICMR APPROVED)
7.	I . Inimai Mercilin Guide Dr . Raj Kishore Mahato	Patients adherence to antihypertensive medication in a tertiary care hospital in Madurai, Tamilnadu (ICMR APPROVED)
8.	Mr. Shreedher Priyan .N Guide Dr . AR.Karthick	Awareness of Cardio-Pulmonry Resuscitation practices and Perspective on Resuscitation Education among Doctors of varied Specialties in Medical College Hospital (ICMR APPROVED)
9.	Dr. Katheresan Jayashree	Dundee ready educational environment measures - development and psychometric testing of an abridge version
10.	Dr. Ramesh .R	Antibiotic resistance patterns in the critically ill

மாவட்டம் 4.12.2016 • தினகரன் • மதுரை 15

லூதியானா மாநாட்டில்

வேலம்மாள் மருத்துவ மாணவருக்கு டாக்டர் மிட்டல் விருது

யோகா பயிற்சி

5) Two ICMR (Indian Council of Medical Research) projects- Short term studentship programme projects in Pharmacology under the guidance of Dr.Vallish and in Anaesthesia under the guidance of Dr.Karthikeyan in the year 2015-16 and 2016-17 repectively .

6) Dr. MITTAL AWARD for the Best Poster presentation in All India Anaesthesia Conference held at Ludhiana, Punjab in 2016 under the guidance of Dr.Selvakumar and Dr. Karthikeyen.

7) Finally Dream come true to wear the Guitar belt on my shoulder (Inspired from Varanam Ayiram film)

8) Author of historical science fiction novel "CODED TRIANGLE" in English and "ஃ – மர்ம மு¬க்கோணங்கள்" which was released by Makkal selvan Vijay Sethupathy, Lyricist Vivek, High Court Justice Hon.Baskaran and Hon. Kulasekaran.

2010 | 2013 | 2018

End Log

23/07/2020

After finishing MBBS, I started working in a private hospital in Thanjavur. It was a very poular hospital and I was posted as a medical officer in the Emergency Room. I learnt a lot from the doctors there and gained work experience. My working time was 7 a.m. to 2 p.m. everyday.

After work, taking a good siesta then preparation for PG NEET exam, playing badminton and cricket with my friends in the evening become my routine life.

One day while I was on duty, I got a call from my mom. She had vomiting and was having mild chest discomfort. I took her to the ER I was at for a check up. Her vitals were normal. The ECG and other tests were also Normal. I decided the pain may be due to gastric issues and sent her home with medication.

That same day, a 60 year old male came to the ER with severe chest pain. I wrote a prescription for loading dose of

T. Aspirin 300
T. Clopilet 300
T. Atorvastatin 80
T. Isodril 20
T.Pan 80

After giving these tablets to the patient , he got relieved from the pain. I had prevented severe cardiac arrest. I handed him over to the intensivist. The patient's relatives held my hands and thanked me for the timely intervention that had saved him. I felt overwhelmed as that feeling was totally new to me.

After my shift got over, I took my bike parked near the pharmacy. I remembered my professors used to say everyone should have the loading dose tablets in their home for emergency use.So I bought a set and kept it in our house.

Two days later, my mother had severe chest pain which was diagnosed to be massive cardiac arrest. I gave her that very loading dose in my house that I had bought the other day and shifted her to my hospital. She was given Heparin injection to dissolve the block in her blood vessels by the intensivist. We then shifted her to a higher center they did thrombolysis procedure.

After the thirty minutes has passed, an ECG was taken and it showed improvement. It was only then I relaxed as I knew my mom was out of danger. She was taken to the ICU and monitored for 24 hours . My dad and I slept in the steps outside the ICU throughout the night.

After the COVID test results came negative, they advised us to do angiography. During the procedure they showed me a 95 percent block in one of the blood vessels in the heart. Angioplasty procedure was done successfully and mom was recovering well.

As a doctor, I knew the importance of those five tablets that saved my mom's life. The story came down to this. All the events that happened from my childhood till now would ultimately lead me to save my mother at right time.

Where does the butterfly theory fit into all this you ask?

If I had missed that Yuvraj singh match in 2004, then I wouldn't have saved my mother and many others life in 2020. Well, if you had connected the dots...

As I saw Yuvraj play cricket, I wanted to be a professional cricketer like him. I went to Don Bosco just for a better playground, switched to Kendriya Vidhyalaya for cricket, then switched to Maxwell to forget cricket. Finally went to Namakkal residential school because I couldn't forget cricket staying back at my home town. Throughout my life, cricket has been the only thing that I was constantly in touch with.

Once a Bachelor of Cricket always a Bachelor of cricket!

I learned just about everything, like passion, love, politics, jealousy, hatred, casteism, common sense, attitude, reality, rejection and lot more from cricket. Somehow these were the subjects in the course of cricket and somehow I had passed it all. And now I am a Bachelor of Cricket.

This part of my story comes to an end, just like my favourite quote!

"Everything ends on a happy note. If it is not happy, then it is not the end "

Sounds far fetched right. Often reality is stranger than fiction.

Hence proved.

There are so many Bachelors of cricket in our country who have worked in different professions just like me. Before the age of 20, you get hit by economical condition, you fail in your passion, your love rejects you. Having crossed all these struggles, life taught me how to be mature.

There was nothing more in life that can depress me. Even though I flay my Namakkal school as a hell hole but it is the only reason for my white coat .It brought out the best of academics part from me ,until unless it is priced by your parents,it is the best place for us to study for the 11th and 12th exams .

The best lesson that I have learnt was “Sometimes your best ball bowled gets on the edge for a four and sometimes it goes on a full toss and gets a wicket. Life is full of uncertainity. Here ends my first innings”.

An artist has a particular type of heart,a particular personality.
It's a different type of life that makes a person an artist.
Take a look at anyone's life.
Musicians,singer, artists,painters,writers.
They all have onething in common.
Which they all definitely have in some form or other.
Pain
Sorrow,Misery,tears.....
Until a person doesn't suffer,he can never make it big.
They all have gone through a lot of pain.
They got hurt,suffered,winced in pain.
When your heart is broken to shattered tiny pieces that's when the music flows.

-Rockstar movie

Author's Desk

Thanks to all those who bought this book and supported me.

Every Novel gets its birth with a question" Why I have to tell this story to everyone ".

Like that my first Novel " Coded Triangles" arised with the question " Why no one taught me about our own Tamil history to me, why the recent generation not even know about our kings like Rajaraja cholan , Rajendhra cholan ".

I wrote that novel with an ambition to develop interest towards the glorious and marvelous Tamil history to our present generation.In the same way this Novel arised with a shout-out angle.

When I joined a college, many of the professors trolled me "Namakal Duck" meaning that students from Namakkal schools are 'Mug up' guys who don't know the concepts as they all skipped their 11th standard portions. They trolled us like we were not capable guys in future. But I want them to understand that Namakkal residential school life is a not a cup of tea ,it takes lot courage and dedication to be there in that residential schools. We the Namakkal school students, all faced lot Physical and Mental stress that these people who eat good food and having good sleep never know.

Starting from morning brushing to Night supper we have to stand in que and even if we are in hunger we have to wait for 'food time', we have to eat whatever hostel gives even if we don't like that, similarly staying away from parents in 15 years old is emotionally not easy for everyone. This needs a lot of mental health.

So I decided to write a Novel with this story line. Hope you all enjoyed my rough and tough crazy roller coaster ride.

"A single happening will not come from a single point rather it comes from a cluster of happenings which finally merge in some other point ".

Eagerly waiting for your reviews

FB -Shreedher priyan
Insta - Priyan666

www.ingramcontent.com/pod-product-compliance
Ingram Content Group UK Ltd.
Pitfield, Milton Keynes, MK11 3LW, UK
UKHW041955190726
13854UKWH00005B/1981

9 798886 061734